Making the Grade

Plucky Schoolmarms of Kittitas Country

Making the Grade

Plucky Schoolmarms of Kittitas Country

BARB OWEN

Washington State University Press
Pullman, Washington

WASHINGTON STATE
UNIVERSITY

Washington State University Press
PO Box 645910
Pullman, Washington 99164-5910
Phone: 800-354-7360
Fax: 509-335-8568
E-mail: wsupress@wsu.edu
Web site: wsupress.wsu.edu

Library of Congress Cataloging-in-Publication Data

Owen, Barb, 1931-
    Making the grade : plucky schoolmarms of Kittitas Country / Barb Owen.
        p. cm.
    Includes bibliographical references and index.
    ISBN 978-0-87422-299-9 (alk. paper)
    1. Women teachers—Washington (State)—Kittitas County—Interviews.
2. Education—Washington (State)—Kittitas County—History—20th century.
I. Title.

    LA2315.W3O94 2008
    371.10092'2--dc22
    [B]

Fine Quality Books from the Pacific Northwest

To Milton Wagy
Local History Librarian extraordinaire

Contents

Acknowledgments

The origin of *Making the Grade* dates from 1998 when I asked my friend, Verna Boedcher Watson, if she would tell me what it was like to teach in a rural one-room schoolhouse back in 1925 and let me tape it. She kindly agreed and even loaned pictures to go with her story. The interview flowed with minimum prompting from me and I found her account lively, fun, and deeply human. Verna was 90, yet her enduring enthusiasm for those long ago years was catching. I could envisage her classroom, those early morning walks in the snow to get the schoolhouse stove going, and her husband-to-be emerging from under a hay baler one autumn afternoon, saying, "Howdy schoolmarm." It was then I discovered what fun this was.

She suggested other teachers, who in turn named others, as did Milton Wagy at the Ellensburg Public Library, Claudia Sikes of the Kittitas County Museum, Lillian Johnson, Senior Activities columnist for the *Ellensburg Daily Record*, and others. After numerous phone calls, missed appointments, failing equipment, and other mishaps, I had collected five other stories from teachers who were still with us.

Luckily for me, there were other excellent teacher interviews in the Ellensburg Public Library archives. A search produced seven done in the 1970s that had sufficient length and were appropriate for inclusion in *Making the Grade*. Now I had 13 delightful stories about rural schools from 1914 to 1942. Most of the teachers had grown up in Ellensburg or rural Kittitas County, and all had attended the Ellensburg Normal School before starting their careers.

The next challenge was to get these tape recorded interviews into print form. When my old word processor wore out I was forced to learn how to use a computer. Much to my delight I found it to be the perfect tool for this work. Only the lively nature of these personal accounts, however, carried this awkward typist through the hard effort of transcribing. I wore out several tape players from subjecting them to constant play/rewind commands essential for transcription before I discovered the transcribing machine.

Nevertheless, my appreciation constantly grew for these independent, strong-willed young women, who often chose to teach in the face of seemingly overwhelming odds.

* * *

I have had many helping hands in searching for relevant recordings, documents, photos, newspapers, files, etc. for the teachers' stories. I relied extensively on the Ellensburg Public Library, which has an exceptionally large and diverse local history collection. Milton Wagy at the library has an awesome memory of its content.

Dieter Aldritch, then director of archives at Central Washington University, Brigid Clift at the Washington State Archives (Central Branch), and Erin Black, director of the Kittitas County Museum, all gave unstintingly of their time. Help was also gladly provided by Marge Boles at the Kittitas Genealogical Society, Andy and Kathy Hickman at Hancock Printing, local historian Colin Condit, Brenda Owens of the Teanaway Grange, and Gerard Hogan and Mari Knirck at the Central Washington University Library. In addition, thanks go to Charlotte McQueen, and to Becky Schnebly, who read parts of the manuscript.

I also want to acknowledge Debby Desoer, director of the Ellensburg Public Library, for permission to publish anything in the library's archives, Jeff Robinson of the *Ellensburg Daily Record* for allowing me to use material from *Hometown Heritage*, and Hilton Grandstaff for permission to utilize his "Memories of Cabin Creek."

Much appreciated encouragement was provided by my family, Cynthia Murray, Janet Adams, the staff at the Ellensburg Public Library, members of Ellensburg's Historical Society, the folks in the Kittitas Valley Unitarian Universalist congregation, and all my friends. A special thank-you also goes to Donna Nylander and Marv and Betty Kelley of the Little Schoolhouse at the Kittitas County Fairgrounds.

I am indebted to the teachers I interviewed and to their relatives for sharing photographs, memoirs, and other memorabilia to flesh out these remarkable reminiscences and for their permission to include the stories in this anthology. Cameo portraits of the young women came from the Washington State Normal School annual, *The Kooltuo*, and from family members.

Frank and Billie Schnebly shared pictures and a memoir that Frank's mother (ELSIE HODGSON SCHNEBLY) had written about her early life. Richard Fischer contributed photos of his mother (FLORENCE FOLTZ FISCHER). Barbara McQueen was indefatigable in supplying illustrations, memoirs, and even a diary, which added greatly to her mother's story (GRACE HANKS McQUEEN). Barbara Brooks also generously furnished photos and a memoir written by her mother (VERNA BOEDCHER WATSON). Elaine Saxby Baker contributed pictures to enhance her mother's story (ETHEL ROBINSON SAXBY), and Patrick Haberman likewise provided a portrait of his mother (Ferne Charlton Haberman).

Permissions to publish the other reminiscences were graciously granted by Ermina Lowe (Marie Pierson Lowe), Ernest Hadley (Helen "Nell" Donald Hadley), Patricia McKnight Starbird (Theresa Mus McKnight), Gerald Haberman (Ruby Gustafson Haberman and Mary Hartman Gustafson), and by Emma Darter Utz and May Spurling Jankowski.

My heartfelt thanks and deep gratitude go to the Washington State University Press Editorial Board, Editor-in-Chief Glen Lindeman, and all the staff for their belief in my book and for their editorial expertise and professional dedication in publishing *Making the Grade*.

Regrettably, there may be many deserving others whom I have failed to remember. Please accept my humble apologies beforehand if this is the case.

Kittitas County School Districts, 1921

Included in the districts list are the names of the schoolmarms and dates where they "first" accepted teaching positions in Kittitas County. After their first year, teachers often moved to other districts. A majority of the schoolhouses were one-room structures. The few that are known (or believed) to have had two or more classrooms are identified by underlined district numbers on the map.

Gaps in the districts' numbering sequence are due to schools that had not formed up or were closed. Note, too, that school locations could move from one site to another within a district (e.g., see #12 in the southeast corner of Kittitas County, where classes at different times were held in buildings at Denmark, Badger Pocket, Hansen, and Hi-Line).

Washington State counties

District # - School Name
1 - Thomas or Wilson Creek
2 - Umptanum
3 - Ellensburg
4 - Fairview
⑤- Dysart (VERNA BOEDCHER WATSON, 1925)
6 - Broadview
7 - Damman
⑨- Ballard (THERESA MUS McKNIGHT, 1925)
⑪- Manastash (MARIE PIERSON LOWE, 1914;
    EMMA DARTER UTZ, 1936)
12 - Denmark, Badger Pocket, Hansen, Hi-Line
13 - Woldale
⑭- Lyons, "Woodpecker College" (MARY HARTMAN
    GUSTAFSON, 1925)
15 - Virden
17 - Teanaway
⑱- Upper Naneum (MAY SPURLING JANKOWSKI, 1939)
⑲- Tarpiscan (ELSIE HODGSON SCHNEBLY, 1914)
⑳- Lower Naneum (GRACE HANKS McQUEEN, 1918;
    FERNE CHARLTON HABERMAN, 1919;
    RUBY GUSTAFSON HABERMAN, 1925)

21 - Boylston
22 - South Cle Elum
23 - Nelson
24 - Roslyn
25 - Cle Elum
26 - Casland
㉘- Easton [Cabin Creek 2 miles out]
    (ETHEL ROBINSON SAXBY, 1926)
29 - Thorp Prairie
30 - Tanum
31 - Rolinger
32 - Bristol
33 - Wymer
34 - Ronald
35 - Ridgeway
36 - Thrall
37 - Dry Gulch or "The Brushy," Sunset
38 - Kittitas
㊴- Cove (FLORENCE FOLTZ FISCHER, 1916)
40 - Peoh Point
44 - Liberty
45 - Thorp
㊾- Roza or Rosa (HELEN "NELL" DONALD
    HADLEY, 1920)

Introduction

A.J. Splawn
Ellensburg Public Library

In late August 1861, a 16-year-old cowboy, A.J. Splawn, first set eyes on the Kittitas Valley: "It... was the loveliest spot I had ever seen—to the west the great Cascade range, to the northwest the needle peaks of the [Peshastin] stood as silent sentinels over the beautiful dell below, where the Yakima wound its way the length of the valley and disappeared down the grand canyon. From the mountains to the north flowed many smaller streams, while the plain was dotted here and there with groves and thickly carpeted with grass. It was truly the land of plenty. Sage hens, jack rabbits and prairie chickens were on all sides; many sweet-throated song birds were warbling their hymns to the departing day, to be followed, a little later by the coyote's howl, echoing from hill to hill...[We wondered] how long before the settler would discover this Eden and we would see the smoke curling from the chimney of his log cabin."[1]

Indeed, Splawn later became a prominent settler, businessman, and politician in central Washington, and eventually a state senator in the Olympia legislature. In 1861, he was participating in a cattle drive north from the Columbia River to the bustling British Columbia gold fields. In a few years, the valley's tall lush grass and plentiful water became a cattleman's paradise. It was a convenient place for stockmen to rest or recoup their herds on long drives north toward Canada or west to the Puget Sound settlements.

For Native Americans, the Kittitas Valley had long been a focal point for trails extending between the Columbia and Snake rivers to the south and the Wenatchee and Okanogan areas to the north, and the Cascade passes on the west and the Columbia Basin to the east. For unknown centuries, northern bands of Yakama Indians occupied the Kittitas country, which provided rich natural resources for seasonal subsistence rounds. During the late fur trade era of the 1840s, the bands owned vast herds of horses, plus numerous cattle acquired in trade with whites. Fur traders and Catholic missionaries also introduced agriculture; consequently Indian families maintained small gardens and sometimes even orchards in central Washington.

Catholic priests at the short-lived Immaculate Conception Mission (1848–49) on Manastash Creek and from the Ahtanum Mission in the

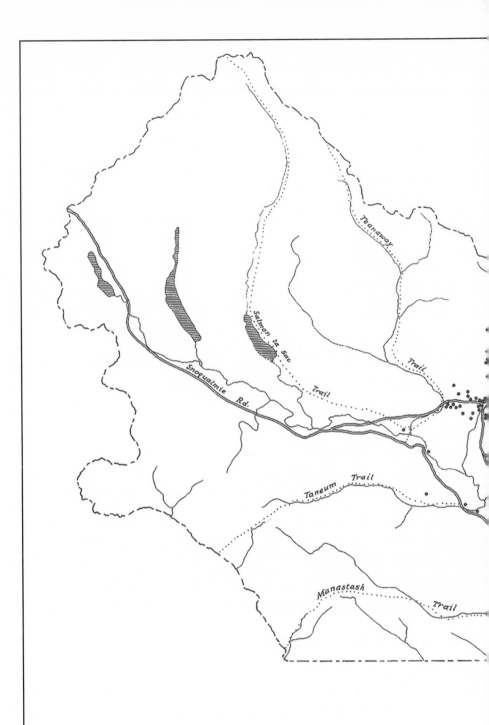

From the *Kittitas County Atlas,* Port Authority of Kittitas County, 1967.
Ellensburg Public Library

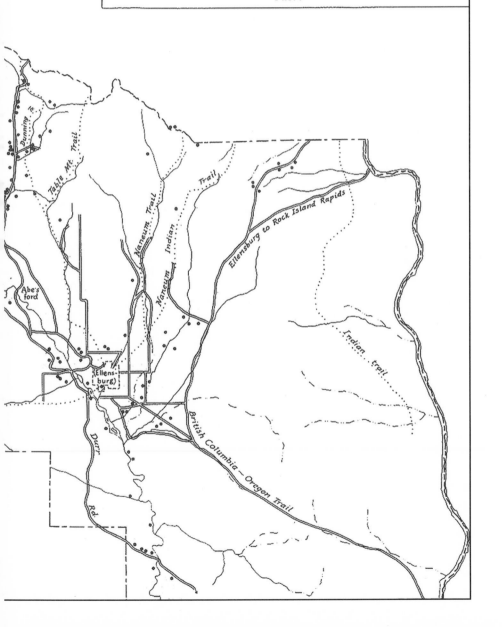

KITTITAS COUNTY

HOMESTEADS, ROADS and TRAILS
1870~1900

Miles

Yakima Valley perhaps introduced some schooling of Kittitas Indian children. These initial efforts, however, would have been cut short during a period of unrest following the signing of the Yakima Treaty in the Walla Walla Valley (June 1855). In the subsequent 1855–58 Yakima War, territorial officials ordered the removal of Catholic priests, as occasional columns of Territorial Militia and U.S. Army troops swept through in pursuit of warriors. There were a few minor clashes between Indians and white miners and soldiers in the Kittitas country, but the major battles occurred elsewhere in the Columbia Plateau region.

When peace was restored, some Indian families still occupied the Kittitas Valley, living on peaceful terms with cattlemen and early settlers. Eventually, most resettled to the Yakama and Colville reservations, and some even to the Nez Perce and Umatilla reserves in Idaho and Oregon. A few Indian families, however, opted not to move and instead took up claims under the Indian Homestead Act.[2] Others, often on excursions from the reservation, would simply camp awhile on lands yet unclaimed by white homesteaders. Small groups of traveling Indian families were a common scene in the Kittitas country for several decades.

Settling the Valley

Viola—the first white child born in the valley, March 1869, daughter of Mr. and Mrs. Charles Splawn.
Ellensburg Public Library

For the early settlers, getting to the Kittitas Valley was the first hurdle. They came on horseback and by foot, guiding pack horses along ancient Indian trails to this key crossroads area. In 1865, two white families, the Rozelles and Harringtons, attempted to establish permanent homes in the valley but ran out of provisions and found themselves unprepared for winter. They were rescued by F.M. Thorp, a cattleman from Moxee, and brought to the warmer Yakima Valley.

In 1867, Frederick Ludi and John Goller arrived from Montana, establishing themselves on the west side of the Yakima River. The Indians befriended the two men, although they also naturally tried to discourage the whites from settling in this ancient tribal homeland. "Snow fall Injun deep," they said. "Awful cold, whites can't stand it."

Ludi noted much less snow on the east side of the river and moved over to the site of present-day Ellensburg in the spring of 1868. He grew peas, beans, cabbages, and other vegetables, proving that the valley was not too cold for agriculture (though, of course, Catholic priests and Indians in the region already had adopted some gardening). Another bachelor, William Wilson, had arrived earlier—about 1866—and perhaps married into an Indian band led by Shushuskin. He had settled on what Ludi named Wilson Creek, in the modern-day Ellensburg vicinity. Described by Ludi as a "worthless fellow," William Wilson may have drowned in 1868 when trying to escape across the Snake River with a band of stolen horses. There are many conflicting stories about his life and death, with some claiming he died as late as 1914.

In June 1868, Tillman Houser, a stockman from Renton in the Puget Sound country, drove 15 cattle over the Cascades and settled in the valley. That August, Charles Splawn, the brother of A.J. Splawn, came to the Taneum Creek area with his wife, the first white woman in the valley. In October, Houser brought his wife, too, plus their three children. Now there were two families and at least two, maybe three, bachelors settled in the Kittitas Valley.

That same year, Charles Splawn and F.M. Thorp established the first postal and express service in the region, hiring an Indian employee to travel weekly to Seattle for $10 a trip. Then in 1869, they established the Taneum Post Office, with Thorp as the first postmaster. (The caption for an old photo of the Thorp-Splawn cabin makes mention of its use as a school,[3] while a few surviving chronicles of the era vaguely refer to it as an

Thorp-Splawn cabin in the Taneum (northwest of Ellensburg)—the first valley post office, birthplace of Viola Splawn, and possibly an "Indian school." *Washington State Archives*

Indian school. There appears, however, to be no confirming record for this.)

The year 1869 saw a significant increase in the number of settlers coming into the valley, no doubt encouraged by a new wagon road completed over Snoqualmie Pass (1867) and the federal government's land survey establishing the township and range grid (1868). Tillman Houser, the pioneer of 1868,

Robber's Roost.
Ellensburg Public Library

was the first to file at a government land office in the spring of 1869. Some people came to stay, while others drifted in and then drifted away again. Some of the stockmen just herded cattle for the summer.

In 1870, A.J. Splawn decided to set up a trading post on a common camping spot—a location that soon became the town of Ellensburgh. A friend with a sense of humor put a sign over the door, "Robber's Roost," and the name stuck. In 1875, John Shoudy from Seattle platted "Ellensburgh," naming it in honor of his wife. Phenomenally quick growth came in the 1880s.

School Development, 1870s to the early 1900s

By 1871, the white population in the Kittitas Valley had increased to 14 families and 35 bachelors, most of them involved in raising livestock. With settlement came the need for schools. As eager as most of the pioneer families were to educate their children, they first had to prove up their claims and take care of basic needs. As one old-timer put it, "It was a time when men concerned themselves with covering up their outsides and filling up their insides." After erecting cabins, barns, corrals, fences, and planting crops, the next priority was education for their children.

In anticipation of future population growth, four large school districts were established in Yakima County, in which the Kittitas Valley then was included (Kittitas County would be created in1883). These designations made schooling "official," but no public money was available for providing facilities or hiring teachers. Two of the districts included portions of the Kittitas country.

Records of the early pioneer schools in the valley are rather sketchy, but nevertheless basic patterns can be discerned.[4] It is was an era of large families, thus most Kittitas Valley schools were taught family style—i.e., children of all ages were gathered together in one room of a home. Parents often served as instructors, but just as often teachers were brought in and the parents paid them by subscription.

Fairview District #4 log cabin school organized by Charles P. Cooke in the early 1870s, and serving to 1891 when replaced by a new structure.
Ellensburg Public Library

When communities began building small public school buildings—to teach all eight grades in one room—it was a natural continuation of the earlier family/home unit type of schooling. Widely scattered one room schools also were the solution to educating the children of families living in sparsely populated areas with primitive roads and other travel limitations.

Some settlers built log cabins on their property to serve as schools. These generally were rough-hewn unheated structures, with a chair and table for the teacher and slab benches mounted on round legs for the students. Typically, school was held only during good weather for a three month term. An exceptional log cabin school—with a half-window and fireplace—stood on the Dysart farm and was considered one of the best in the valley. While most of the early schools were short-lived, there still was a Dysart School in 1925 when VERNA BOEDCHER WATSON taught there, though probably in a more up to date building.

In those days, the books used by children were whatever they could bring from home (perhaps books that the parents had saved from their own school years), or whatever a teacher might bring. Teachers and parents had to be resourceful. Primers were often made by the mothers. Paper was folded and sewn-bound on the spine to form a book, and then the pages were pasted with letters, words, and pictures cut from magazines and newspapers. One teacher drew her own maps on brown butcher paper, painting them with water colors. She also made a globe with a ball of carpet warp, covering it with white cloth and painting in the continents. In 1877, the parents of children in the Reed School sent for schoolbooks costing $10 a set.[5] This was quite a bit of money for those times, but the books could be shared by all the children in the family.

In 1873, gold discoveries in the Swauk region just north of the valley brought more people into the region, in addition to the settlers arriving to

Gold miners.
Ellensburg Public Library

take up agricultural pursuits in the valley. The Stepp School was built on a road that ran from Ellensburgh north to the Swauk and Peshastin gold mines. A former student there recalled having men teachers most of the time.

By 1879, there were nine school districts in the valley, and a little public school money had begun flowing in from the county seat in Yakima. It was never enough to adequately pay teachers, however, and the parents had to make up the balance.

The 1880s were years of rapid growth in the valley. From 1881 to 1884, the population of Ellensburgh (incorporated 1883) increased from 50 to 450, while the number of school districts in the county went up to 19. Improvements continued to be made on the wagon trail across Snoqualmie Pass, and a stage line was established between The Dalles and Ellensburgh, while cattle baron Ben Snipes opened Ellensburgh's first bank. In 1885, the first community fair was held and the county population stood at 2,751.

In 1882, Ellensburgh's first public schoolhouse had been built with private funds at a cost of $2,500, all raised by subscription. It was a 35' x 70' two-story wood structure with two classrooms—one for primary children and the other for intermediate students. A principal also was appointed. The initial three-month term opened in September. The school operated with three sessions a year, charging parents $3 per term. An 1883 report stated that 50 students were enrolled, with an average attendance of 30 percent (measles had cut into attendance).

In 1884, the Presbyterian Church bought the building and turned the first floor into the Ellensburgh Academy, which offered a grades 1–12 curriculum. The academy operated for a decade. The public school, in the meantime, continued to be held upstairs.

The county's population continued to experience record growth from 1885 to 1890, increasing by about 6,000 to 8,761. Ellensburgh itself had expanded by about 2,250 residents, with an 1890 census count of 2,758. (Eventually, the earlier spelling of "Ellensburgh" officially gave way to "Ellensburg" in 1894, when the U.S. Postal Service dropped the "h.")

It appears that another privately funded public school was being planned[6] to replace the inadequate upstairs location in the Ellensburgh Academy when a disastrous fire on July 4, 1889, leveled the town—10 business blocks and many homes were destroyed. With typical pioneer spirit, the townspeople immediately began rebuilding, focusing on erecting safer brick and stone structures. Even if the newly planned public

Washington School.
Ellensburg Public Library

Washington School, Room 1, February 22, 1896.
Ellensburg Public Library

school had escaped destruction, the city fathers probably were concerned about the fire hazard in regard to a wooden structure. In 1890, local voters passed a $50,000 bond issue to build Ellensburgh's Washington School, the first public educational facility in the town paid for with taxpayer money. The three story brick structure stood on Fifth Street and probably offered a nine month school term.

Not long after statehood in 1889, the legislature in Olympia selected Ellensburgh as one of three locations in Washington hosting a State Normal School, with the other two communities being Cheney and New Whatcom (Bellingham). Normal schools were modeled on the French *école normale*, specifically offering teacher training in a shorter and more effective curriculum than the traditional, small, and often exclusive private four-year denominational colleges of the time. In 1891, the Normal School in Ellensburgh began offering classes on the top floor of the Washington School. Barge Hall, the first instructional and administrative building on the new campus north of town, would be completed in 1894.

In that same year, there were 2,419 school age children in the county, with 1,770 of them enrolled in 36 school districts under the direction of 44 teachers. One room schools, of course, predominated in the rural localities and were situated within walking distance in their respective farming family districts. Interestingly enough, the Kittitas County School Superintendent reported a broad range of term offerings from 1891 to 1902—with some districts averaging only 3 months per year, and others offering as much as 10–11 months a year.

Between 1900 and 1903, the average school term in Kittitas County was 6.4 months, but an increasing number of schools offered at least 9 months. Between 1904 and 1908, average term lengths grew to 7 months. By 1909, it was 8.2 months, slowly rising to 9.1 months in 1922–23.

The Northern Pacific Railroad and Prosperity

The arrival of the Northern Pacific, the first transcontinental railway to reach Washington, was a key factor in the growth of Kittitas County. The first NP train arrived in Ellensburgh from Yakima in early 1886, after workers battled with winter runoff along newly laid tracks in the Yakima

Trestle construction in the Stampede Pass locality, ca. 1886–87.
Kittitas County Historical Museum

Canyon. Ellensburgh was elated, but the NP still had the grueling task of laying tracks across the Cascade Range and completing the link to Tacoma on Puget Sound.

The NP decided on an elaborate set of switchbacks over Stampede Pass until an expensive tunnel was completed. The switchbacks were ready by June 1, 1887, and used until the new tunnel opened for rail traffic on May 27, 1888. Within months, ongoing problems developed with the tunnel, thus the switchbacks often served as an essential backup.[7]

Meanwhile, permanent repair shops and a roundhouse for the division were established at Ellensburgh, providing a boon to the city. The *Ellensburgh Capital* later reported: "The crews of trains, repairmen and maintenance men swelled the population by several hundred! A large part of the monthly payroll of $30,000 to $50,000 was spent locally."[8]

Early coal mining.
Ellensburg Public Library

So began a period of high hopes for Ellensburgh and the Kittitas Valley. The western part of the county also participated in this surge of prosperity. NP officials had noticed showings of coal in the Cle Elum/Roslyn district. Upon closer investigation, they found major deposits of high-grade, non-clinkering coal of a type ideal for steam locomotives. The Northern Pacific Coal Company, a subsidiary of the NP, founded the Roslyn town site and 500 laborers soon were working in the new mines. In 1887, Roslyn's first school opened on Dakota Street in a vacant building owned by the coal company. It mostly operated on subscriptions from the miner families.

Forests of the eastern Cascade foothills also yielded immense wealth, as workers flowed to new sawmills and lumber camps. In 1886, the Cle Elum School District was formed, with the Reed cabin serving as the schoolhouse and the teachers boarding at the Reed Hotel. Teachers were paid by subscription.

Along with the NP's substantial payroll, Kittitas County also benefited from relatively low railway transportation costs for hauling the valley's crops, grain, hay, livestock, and dairy products. A new era in farming and ranching began as rural residents took advantage of the increased access to Puget Sound markets. Miners in the Okanogan country, too, relied on Ellensburgh, as it was the nearest town of any size with a railway connection. The city became a key outfitting center for the northern mines.

Upper Kittitas County sawmill.
Ellensburg Public Library

Meanwhile, new immigrants, businessmen, company officials, financiers, professional people, tourists, politicians, and celebrities continued to arrive in bustling Ellensburgh. Hastily erected hotels, restaurants, banks, shops, and even an opera house opened to serve the burgeoning tide of humanity. Additions to the city were platted and sold, as real estate values soared.

For many, the sudden prosperity went to their heads—they began believing anything was possible. Resurgent talk arose about "immense" iron deposits

Northern Pacific roundhouse.
Ellensburg Public Library

Electricity, 1887–1930s

In 1882, S.Z. Mitchell, a student of Thomas Edison, eagerly headed west to capitalize on his mentor's newly developed steam-generated electrical technology. By 1887, John Shoudy, a local pioneer and visionary, had contracted Mitchell to set up an Edison system for lighting Ellensburgh's streets. The

Hydroelectric power plant on the Yakima River. *Ellensburg Public Library*

resulting steam plant generated enough power for 50 arc street lights and 300 Edison incandescent bulbs that lit up some stores and all the hotels. Four years later, the citizens of Ellensburgh passed a $44,000 bond issue to purchase the plant, and in 1904, as electrical demand continued to grow, they approved another bond issue authorizing a new hydroelectric plant on the Yakima River.

By the early 1920s, the Ellensburg City Electric Utility ran out of capacity and turned to Puget Sound Power and Light (PSPL had operated in the Cle Elum area since 1917, when it supplied power to electric-powered trains on the Milwaukee Road). In 1925, the Ellensburg utility sold off their rural customers to PSPL and signed a contract to purchase additional power from the company. Meanwhile, a number of rural residents had established cooperative generators to make their own electricity, until PSPL finally bought them out in the 1930s. Throughout this period, however, electrical power lines were slow in coming to country schools, and indeed to many rural localities.

in the county. Fevered imaginations saw Ellensburgh becoming the Pittsburgh of the west, with extensive mines, furnaces, and rolling mills, which in turn would open up many other manufacturing possibilities. As one local pessimist put it, however, "The boomers boomed and the suckers sucked."

By the start of 1889, with statehood for Washington on the horizon, local citizens dared to dream that Ellensburgh would become the state capital. In the midst of a booming economy and flushed with prosperity and hopes for the future, two local entrepreneurs—the Craig brothers—even built a regal governor's mansion on "Capitol Hill," overlooking the town. Meanwhile, real estate developers laid out "State Capital Park" just north of Ellensburgh and surrounded it with platted residential lots.

The Washington constitutional convention in 1889 decided to have the citizenry choose a location for the state capital. Campaigning among the

Ellensburgh's Masonic Temple, destroyed in the July 4, 1889, conflagration.
Ellensburg Public Library

contenders proceeded in earnest, with Ellensburgh maintaining that the capital should be located in the center of the state. Also, Ellensburgh boasted of a larger population base than either of the other two main contenders, Yakima and Olympia, and claimed it soon would be the largest commercial and manufacturing city in the state.

And then suddenly—the bottom dropped out. Cracks leading to the "bottom" started on July 4, 1889, when the disastrous fire destroyed most of Ellensburgh's downtown business district. Undaunted, the citizens started to cleanup and rebuild "as soon as the ashes were cool." When the governor wired to ask the mayor what Ellensburgh needed, the reply was, "The

Ellensburgh in August 1890, recovering from the great fire of the previous year. The "Governor's mansion" stands at left in this scene from "Capitol Hill."
University of Washington Libraries (UW11912)

Capital!" More currently required, though, was money for the rebuilding effort. Initially funds readily came in, but then dwindled as Ellensburgh's prospects for the capital dimmed.

In statewide elections on October 1, 1889, vote tallies showed Yakima at 14,711, Ellensburgh with 12,833, and Olympia, the old territorial capital, at 25,490. Olympia led, but not with a clear majority as required. Yakima and Ellensburgh's combined tally of 27,544 votes later suggested to "hind-sighters" that the capital could have been located in central Washington, if the two cities had united their efforts on one community or the other. In Ellensburgh, hopes flagged and real estate values slumped or disappeared. The next vote in November 1890 gave the capital to Olympia with a majority count of 37,413.[9]

Panic of 1893 and Recovery for a New Century

By the early 1890s, record business losses following the calamitous fire, the contentious failure to gain the state capital, a Roslyn coal mine disaster, the closure of Ben Snipes' Roslyn and Ellensburgh banks, a three year drought, and dwindling farm incomes did not dim the pioneers' faith in the future, as evidenced by the local bond issues they passed. The Panic of 1893, however, delivered the coup de grace.

The severe depression years, 1893–96, affected urban and rural citizens, both nationally and internationally. The causes were many, including agricultural depression, farm mortgage problems, reckless railway financing, and unsound banking practices. Commercial stagnation in Europe forced international investors to curb the flow of capital into the United States. Farms collapsed under heavy mortgage payments, and the banks in turn were unable to find buyers for the foreclosed properties. As businesses, railroads, and banks failed in record numbers, investment was greatly restricted, and income and profits drastically declined. The overall economy suffered from a low consumption of goods.

Threshing crew, 1898.
Ellensburg Public Library

Roslyn School, 1906. Substantial numbers of Black Americans and a host of additional ethnic groups and nationalities were drawn to the coal mines for the employment opportunities.
Ellensburg Public Library

"Twenty-four different nationalities attending school at Roslyn, Wash.," 1913. First row (l. to r.) Frank Giovanni, Italian; unidentified, Scotch; Frank Ross, Czechoslovakian; unidentified; Mihelich boy, Croatian; unidentified; unidentified, French. Second row—unidentified; "Pitch" Schwab, Russian; Johnson boy, Finnish; unidentified; unidentified; Adams boy, Dalmatian (Yugoslavian); Morgan boy, English. Third row—Johnson girl, Finnish; Fomia Wakin, Syrian; unidentified; Hanna Green, African; Juline Mc…, Irish; unidentified. Fourth row—Frances Mihelich, Croatian; Alice Nelson, Swedish; John Berg, German; Booth boy; Audrey Cusworth, Welsh.
Ellensburg Public Library

Eventually, recovery came in 1897 with banking consolidation, a strong return of foreign investments, and the revived export of manufacturing goods and farm products, creating a positive net balance of payments. A reemphasis on gold also prompted increased prospecting; the Yukon Gold Rush influenced Seattle's emergence from the depression.

Improved agricultural equipment and farming methods increased production and brought in much needed revenue to help pull Kittitas County out of the hard times. Though the Klondike excitement drew off miners to Alaska, the population of Kittitas County continued to grow. During the Spanish-American War period and the subsequent opening of new Asian markets, high prices for commodities fully revived the economy in the valley.[10]

Along with the rest of the nation, Kittitas County entered the new century on a surge of prosperity, with expanding population, services, and innovations. Electricity became more common, the telephone more widely used, the first automobile crossed Snoqualmie Pass in 1905, and a new transcontinental railway came to the county (the Milwaukee Road, 1909).

Between 1903 and 1910, the county population grew from 9,704 to 18,561, but then would remain fairly steady for the next three decades. The number of school districts in town and country peaked at 44 in 1915. Meanwhile, improvements were being made in teacher training, facilities, salaries, instructional materials, school term length, government support, and access to education, but changes in the rural schools often lagged well behind those in town schools.

A promise of increased farm prosperity had come with the construction of three irrigation canals bringing water from the Cascade slopes. In the early 1900s, the Cascade Canal, Town Ditch, and West Side Ditch irrigated more than 26,000 acres in the Kittitas Valley. The largest project would be the Kittitas Reclamation District's High

Irrigation canal dredging.
Ellensburg Public Library

Line Canal, begun in 1911 and completed in 1920. More acres under irrigation resulted in more prosperity for farmers, eventually meaning more support for rural schools. The number of country schools peaked at 36 in this period.

Snoqualmie Pass, 1916.
Ellensburg Public Library

The first horseless carriages appeared in Washington in 1900—one each in Seattle and Spokane. Kittitas County, along with the rest of the nation, eagerly embraced motorized vehicles and soon began improving roadways to accommodate them. By 1906, there were 763 vehicles statewide and 1,200 miles of highway. Yakima raised its speed limit from 6 mph to 12 mph, even before Seattle did. In 1915, state highway miles increased to 37,500 with an accompanying increase in the number of automobiles. In parts of rural Kittitas County, however, there were few if any motorized vehicles or adequate roadways. In those areas, everyone still rode horseback, such as ELSIE HODGSON SCHNEBLY when she taught in the Tarpiscan and Brushy districts along the Columbia River in 1914–16.

Prohibition came to Kittitas County in 1915, lasting until 1933. As was typical in many areas in those days, an illegal and lucrative underground business developed in the making and selling of "moonshine" whisky. No doubt, the teachers in *Making the Grade* knew that "bootlegging" was common in rural Kittitas County, but only one of them made any mention of alcohol. ELSIE HODGSON SCHNEBLY probably summed up a typical attitude, saying she would "never dance with a man who had anything to drink."

Washington State Normal School, Ellensburg

In the teachers' reminiscences in *Making the Grade*, all mentioned their training at the Washington State Normal School, often including fond memories of the time spent there in the 1910s–1930s period. The Normal School had opened on September 6, 1891, in four rooms on the second floor of the Washington School. Four faculty members greeted 51 students, with the minimum age for admission being 15 for women and 16 for men.

Initially, the curriculum was an ambitious three-year teacher training program. In the earliest years, admission rules required an enrollee to have at least passed the Washington State Eighth Grade Examination, but exceptions

Barge Hall opened on the new WSNS campus in 1894.
Ellensburg Public Library

From Teachers College to University

1891—Washington State Normal School (WSNS)

1937—Central Washington College of Education (CWCE)

1961—Central Washington State College (CWSC)

1976—Central Washington University (CWU)

eventually were made. In some years, applicants could take an equivalent on-site test at the Normal School and gain admission. At one time WSNS offered 9th grade. Also, some applicants who were over the age of 20 with business "or equivalent" experience and who were deemed to be good bets for becoming teachers, regardless of scholarship, could be admitted.

Generally, if admitted with an eighth grade diploma or equivalent status, a student followed the first set of education courses for three years and then became eligible for employment with a Two Year Teaching Certificate. Another set (the Advanced Course) called for three years of study. Generally, if students entered with one, two, or more years of high school, they could start in the Advanced Course and graduate with a diploma good for five years of teaching. If these graduates successfully taught in schools for two to five years, they could earn a Life Diploma.[11]

In the same time period, the state legislature also authorized The Agricultural College, Experiment Station and School of Science of the State of Washington (today's Washington State University, Pullman) and provided a revitalized new beginning for the previously established University of Washington (Seattle). These efforts, along with the creation of the Normal Schools at Ellensburgh, Cheney, and New Whatcom (Bellingham), were all part of an ambitious plan to greatly expand advanced educational opportunities for the "masses." In addition to government funds, all five educational institutions were subsidized with ownership of vast acreages of state or federal land.

Ellensburgh Academy, grades 1–12.
Ellensburg Public Library

In 1892, Washington was barely out of the frontier stage and only had a few academies (such as the Ellensburgh Academy) and three "accredited" high schools (in Seattle, Tacoma, and Spokane) to prepare students for collegiate work. Consequently, students with considerably less education than a high school degree were admitted to the Normal Schools. Even the high school graduates attending the Pullman and Seattle institutions often needed to enter a Preparatory program on the campuses before actually taking their first "college" classes. By the late 1910s, when accredited high schools finally had expanded to communities across the state, applicants to each of Washington's Normal Schools were expected to hold high school diplomas.

In 1894, the Ellensburgh college moved into the recently completed Barge Hall, an imposing edifice on the new campus. In the years following the Normal School's founding, however, the curriculum had to be adjusted frequently to address a growing shortage of qualified teachers as the state's population quickly expanded. Eventually a complex variety of one, two, and three year certificates and diplomas with different requirements were made available to aspiring teachers. As an example, the Normal School's 1915 catalog stated, "Those who wish to obtain a certificate authorizing them to teach as early as possible may secure an elementary certificate upon the satisfactory completion of one year's work." Another catalog stated that a vote of the faculty could issue a temporary teaching certificate to those students not completing the full course, but who would eventually continue their training.

Applicants with only eighth grade educations were routinely admitted until 1917, after which time the state legislature required a high school diploma, or equivalent, for admission. That same year, President Black (who served from 1917 to 1931) changed the focus of the college, introducing courses in one room school methods and rural studies to attract those students wishing to become country school teachers. Practice teaching was switched to active schools as well as the Training School. Finally, four basic certificate/diploma routes were established.[12]

In 1925, enrollment stood at about 500 students, with 286 of them receiving the elementary diploma for their two years of study. In 1939, when the last teacher in *Making the Grade* started at the Upper Naneum School, three and four year programs were proscribed.

An early student at the Normal School, Edith McMurry Ellexson, later wrote a delightful campus recollection for the same time period when the first teachers in *Making the Grade* enrolled at the institution. With slight modification, here is Ellexson's account:

> **Stella Stadtler, 1928**
>
> I remember the revolving door at a north entrance (of Barge Hall). The steps were worn down three inches in the spot where people naturally put their feet passing in and out.
>
> The library was in a first-floor room in the "Ad" building (Barge Hall), in a circular room at the south east corner.
>
> I slept on a sleeping porch built on the roof of Kamola. We reached it by climbing out our window. At night we could hear the "silk train" of the Milwaukee Railroad. The high-pitched whistle of the electrified railroad was an eerie sound at night. We were told that the silk trains traveled faster than the other trains. They were carrying expensive loads, and the insurance was less if they were fast.
>
> We attended the Chautauqua [talks] held in a big tent in a play field just north of the Ad Building. The smell of the hot tent holding damp people on mashed grass is still memorable. We usually listened to the music at the beginning, then slipped out under the tent and away to cooler spots.—from *Central Remembered* (1992).

"In 1912, fresh from the 9th grade of a small school in the Cascade Mountains, with no finances, but a great burning desire and ambition to be a schoolteacher, I chose Ellensburg Normal School just 70 miles on the railroad from home.

"With my few belongings, I landed at the gorgeous NP depot and went straight to the office of President Wilson. He was so kind, courteous, and understanding to this 16-year-old country girl that I forgot I was alone, so far from home. He sent me to the home of a wonderful family to work for my room and board. Registration was free but tuition was $10, $5 of which was returnable. At this time there were 10 men teachers and 13 lady teachers and only 265 students…There were 13 men in the whole school, enough for two 5-men basketball teams.

"Assemblies were frequent and were always opened with a reading from the Bible; a hymn was sung, and the Lords Prayer was recited in unison. The study of the Bible was an elective course. P.E. was Physical Culture and we were told it went hand in hand with elocution, which was supposed to give us effective expression of ourselves in attitude, voice, and speech.

"Eighth Street in front of the Normal School was muddy and full of ruts in the wet weather. Across 8th Street was a marsh full of cattails and water fowl, mostly ducks, where they waited for the crumbs we brought. This was Wilson Creek. The Pearl Street sidewalk was all wood. On their way to the loading platform at the railroad track, the cowboys dearly loved driving their sheep down 8th Street where they could flirt with the girls in the newly opened dormitory—Kamola Hall.

"When I entered W.S.N.S. there were two buildings, the Normal School (Barge Hall) and the Training School (Edison Hall), and then there was the newly completed dormitory. This new dormitory accommodated 54 students, but men could also come over for meals. Mrs. Arthur was the housemother and an outstanding lady she was. There was a compulsory study hour.

"Prior to this time the only publication was a small paper called *The Outlook*. This year, 1912–13, they decided on a year book, so they just reversed "Outlook" backwards and called it *Kooltuo*, which was a gorgeous publication with suede leather binding.

"Our social life was fantastic—hayrack rides, picnics on the Yakima River—and we always went to the river for the thrill of seeing loggers with their pike poles walking on the fast moving logs, pushing them away from the bank. When the snow and ice came, there was skating on the river and ponds. The

Geraldine Brain Siks, 1930

I recall, so well, Philosophy Professor William Stephens' use of dramatization in making more understandable the complexities of philosophical meaning. In a corner of the classroom he had collected an impressive assortment of robes, wigs, beards, hats, and materials, which he drew upon in creating his improvisations. I vividly remember his arranging white sheets, as togas, on himself and a class student to depict Socrates and a pupil in philosophical discourse. Wading into the Aegean Sea, Socrates suddenly thrust the student's head under the waters, resolutely holding it there. At last releasing the young man, by then gasping for air, the teacher admonished him: "One can philosophize only when the search for knowledge becomes as essential as breathing."—from *Central Remembered* (1992).

wind was always quite wild and the fashions of the day were hobble skirts, the long skirt with a slit up the side to give longer steps, and the full skirt which nearly caused us to grow humpbacked to keep them from blowing over our heads. Pants or jeans were unheard of. If anyone had dared to wear them they would have been asked to leave the campus immediately."[13]

Rural Schools, 1910s–1930s

Original school wood stove, installed in the relocated Manastash School on the Kittitas County Fairgrounds, Ellensburg. *Barb Owen*

The rural schoolhouse in the early decades of the 20th century was typically a wood clapboard structure—the log cabin schools were practically all gone by then. Normally, the building had but one classroom (though occasionally two rooms), with tall windows along the side walls, student cloakrooms inside the front entrance with shelves for storing lunches, and a wood/coal storage room and often a kitchenette at the other end of the building. Water for drinking and washing was provided either from a pump by the cloakroom or was brought in from an outside source in a pail (with dipper). Rows of student desks faced toward the teacher's desk up front. A large stove, providing heat, stood in the center of the room or at some other appropriate location.

Outside were two small outhouses—one for the boys and one for girls. Even in the late 1930s, outdoor toilets were common. A school north of Ellensburg where MAY SPURLING JANKOWSKI started teaching in 1939 still had outdoor toilets, as did the farms in that particular locality. Some schools also had small horse barns for those students arriving by buggy or on horseback.

A teacher was responsible for cleaning a schoolhouse, and starting the stove and keeping the room heated during classes. In the colder months, a teacher often hired an eighth grade boy to come an hour early to fire up the stove, so that the schoolroom was warm when the other students arrived. At the end of classes, the children often enjoyed pitching in with the teacher and getting the school ready for the next day. The students were from farmhouses or little crossroads communities located within a few miles radius of a schoolhouse. Most everyone, teacher included, walked to school (some came by horseback or buggy), even in the winter. When deep snow or extremely

Denmark School, District #12, near the town of Kittitas, ca. 1898–99. Many teachers started in rural districts with hopes of someday getting employment in town schools.
Ellensburg Public Library

cold temperatures made walking too difficult or hazardous, parents arranged to transport their children by horse-drawn wagons or sleds, or by trucks or automobiles in later years.

Typically, there was no electricity. Schoolroom lighting was provided by natural daylight coming through the tall windows and by gas lamps. Normally, rural classes began at 9 a.m. and ended around 3:30 p.m., thus the students headed home before it got dark. Gas lamps, of course, were required when students and families gathered for evening programs and activities.

Many schoolrooms had large blackboards, pull down maps, and maybe even a globe. Outdoor playground equipment and small libraries were purchased by funds raised at community events. The farthest outlying schools, however, tended to be more primitive and had less of everything.

Judging from the reminiscences presented in *Making the Grade* and by facts in other sources, enrollment in a typical rural schoolhouse during the 1914–20 period was around 15. By 1925–26, the average more likely stood at about two dozen. But even in the 1930s, enrollments could be quite small in some schools. In 1939, MAY SPURLING JANKOWSKI had a grand total of 7 students in the Upper Naneum School.

Regarding the length of school terms, ELSIE HODGSON SCHNEBLY was hired for 6 months at remote Tarpiscan near the Columbia River in 1914. The following year, she started a 9 month term at the Sunset School, but only

Rules for Schoolteachers, 1915

- You will not marry during the term of your contract.
- You are not to keep company with men.
- You must be home between the hours of 8 p.m. and 6 a.m. unless attending school functions.
- You may not loiter downtown in any of the ice cream stores.
- You may not travel beyond the city limits unless you have the permission of the chairman of the board.
- You may not ride in a carriage or automobile with any man unless he is your father or brother.
- You may not smoke cigarettes.
- You may not dress in bright colors.
- You must wear at least two petticoats.
- Your dresses must not be any shorter than two inches above the ankle.
- To keep the school neat and clean, you must: sweep the floor at least once daily; scrub the floor at least once a week with hot, soapy water: clean the blackboards at least once a day: and start the fire at 7 a.m. so the room will be warm by 8 a.m.

taught for 6 months when the small district's money ran out. Teachers more commonly taught a regular 9 month school session. Not all of the students, however, were able to attend a full term, particularly the older boys who needed to work on family farms in stretches during the autumn and spring.

The one and two room schools typically offered instruction in all eight grades. Often enough, there were sufficient numbers of students in a district to fill each grade. On the other hand, this was not the case in schools with a particularly small enrollment. In 1914, MARIE PIERSON LOWE had only

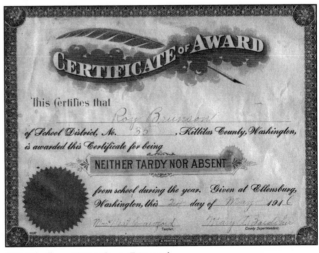

Little Schoolhouse, Kittitas County Fairgrounds

6 students at the remote Manastash School—1 in the third grade, 2 in the seventh grade, and 3 in the eighth grade. Sometimes a teacher would start the

We feel both glad and sad to-day
And scarce can hide the rising tear
We're glad for changes on life's way
Yet sad to part from schoolmates dear

End of school year souvenir, Umptanum.
Ellensburg Public Library

year with a full complement of students, only to have a family move away and the school losing 4 or 5 pupils. Most students came from families owning farms and ranches, or from a hired hand's family. In the peripheral areas bordering the agricultural heart of the Kittitas Valley, additional students came from mining, milling, and lumbering localities.

Many teachers had the added challenge of instructing some older students; these bigger teenage boys frequently spent weeks or months absent from the classroom when working on the family farm. At age 16 or 17, some were resentful about still attending school and making up for lost time. Another particular challenge for teachers involved preparing their eighth graders for the difficult Washington State examinations. Up to the 1930s, students were required to pass these tests in order to advance to high school (see Appendix: Eighth Grade Examination).

The Great Flu Epidemic

As World War I reached a climax in the autumn of 1918, a worldwide flu epidemic began cutting down American adults of all ages, especially healthy young men and women in their 20s and 30s working in factories and extractive industries, living in cities and rural areas, and serving in the armed forces. The exact place of origin remains obscure, but people of the times tagged it the "Spanish Flu," though this may be a misnomer.

The flu arrived in the state of Washington about September 17 with naval recruits from Philadelphia—11 of them already ill. A week later, influenza was of epidemic proportion in Seattle. By October 11, schools were closed and public gatherings prohibited in Seattle, Bremerton, Sultan, Port Angeles, Pasco, Prosser, and Spokane.

In the Kittitas Valley, the influenza passed swiftly through neighborhoods, affecting everyone in some manner. Families were quarantined and schools closed for many weeks. Throughout Kittitas County, friends and family members died. In her diary on December 4, GRACE HANKS McQUEEN noted 70 cases of the flu among Ellensburg High School students. In January and February 1919, she lost four good friends her own age. In the spring of 1919, the virus ran its course, leaving 675,000 dead nationwide and perhaps 30 to 40 million worldwide.

Fan dance in a school program, 1897.
Ellensburg Public Library

In many communities, a schoolhouse served as the social center for hosting box socials, dances, literary readings, war bond drives (during World War I), and other public meetings. A schoolhouse frequently had a kitchenette and perhaps even a little stage at one end of the room. The usual purpose of a box social was to raise money to buy playground equipment or library books. Meals in highly decorated boxes or baskets were prepared beforehand by the local women. Then at the schoolhouse, men made bids for the boxes and baskets, which usually included fried chicken, potato salad, fruit, and pie or cake. A young man might be clued-in as to who prepared which particular box and then he would bid accordingly. Some teachers recalled meeting their future husbands this way. VERNA BOEDCHER WATSON and others noted that the teacher's box usually sold for the highest price. She also remembered the happiness at these events, with couples talking and laughing as they ate box lunches.

Several times a year, teachers prepared their students for special performances— a "program." Presented before parents and others from the local populace, these were important events in rural communities and normally held during the holiday seasons, particularly around Christmastime. District rules often required it, as well as an end-of-year school picnic for students and families. In holiday and springtime programs, students sang, performed short plays, gave

Dressed for a school play, ca.1925.
Ellensburg Public Library

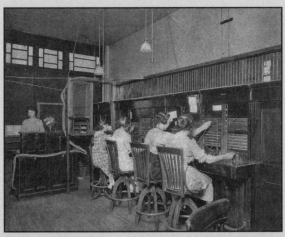

Telephone system workers in Ellensburg: (l. to r.) Jane Yantis, Martha Becker, Mae Morris, Irma Sterling, and Helen Martin.
Merle Ringer

Early Telephone Service

The Sunset Telephone and Telegraph Company first began operating in Ellensburgh circa 1890. By 1900, there were 130 telephones in the county, and 1,600 by 1930. In rural areas, however, the availability of telephone service probably depended on whether or not local farmers and ranchers installed their own lines. In 1914, when ELSIE HODGSON SCHNEBLY taught in a remote area along the Columbia River, she was grateful to have a phone line even if it was just a wire stretched along some fence posts. In the same year, MARIE PIERSON LOWE teaching in the isolated Manastash Canyon recalled how lonely she was with the nearest telephone four miles away. Phone service in rural school areas apparently became more common in the 1920s and certainly so by the late 1930s.

recitations, and danced. The reminiscences in *Making the Grade* make frequent mention of programs. Only one of the teachers, MARIE PIERSON LOWE, did not prepare a program and that was just in one year, 1914–15. Her isolated Manastash School only had six children—too few to do so.

Teachers were much respected in a community, even on a par with doctors and preachers according to MARY HARTMAN GUSTAFSON. Teachers were required to visit each of the students' homes once a year, meeting with the parents and often staying overnight. The girls often argued over who got to sleep next to teacher.

A teacher could expect a superintendent's visit at least once a year, sometimes more, except in hard-to-reach areas where a superintendent might never

An upper county May Day pole dance, ca. 1910.
Ellensburg Public Library

come at all. Local board members, of course, commonly interacted with instructors. Teachers had to remain unmarried if they wanted to keep their jobs, a strict rule that only started changing sometime in the 1930s. The teaching careers of a number of the women in *Making the Grade* eventually ended, or were interrupted, when they met young men and got married. Another was secretly married in the 1920s before the end of her school year term (when interviewed seven decades later, she made me promise not to include this fact in her story—a promise I kept). In 1936, EMMA DARTER UTZ was a married woman when she taught at the Manastash School but by then no one made anything of it.

By the 1930s, the number of active rural schoolhouses dwindled as school busses efficiently transported students on improved roadways to schools located in larger towns—Ellensburg, Kittitas, Cle Elum, and Thorp. The days when parents personally funded a local school were long gone; now schools were public tax-based educational units. In choosing consolidation, parents recognized the county's financial burden in maintaining so many separate schools in the countryside, and they were aware of the perceived educational inequalities of rural institutions as compared to town schools with their better facilities and financing. The one room school was on its way out.[14]

Seventh-grade report card, ca. 1900.
Little Schoolhouse, Kittitas County Fairgrounds

Schoolbooks

In the earlier years of the 20th century, textbooks used in rural schoolhouses often were only what the children could bring from home, just as in the schools of the previous century. When Elsie Hodgson Schnebly started teaching in an isolated location near the Columbia River in 1914, she only had the books she brought with her and a dusty set of geography books left in the school. The parents of the children still had to buy textbooks, or provide a student with books that the family passed down from child to child. This was true even in rural schools much closer to towns. Not until around 1925 did districts start furnishing books.

Today, many examples of these textbooks are archived with the Little Schoolhouse restoration at the Kittitas County Fairgrounds in Ellensburg (see list in Bibliography). Representative examples are included in the following discussion.

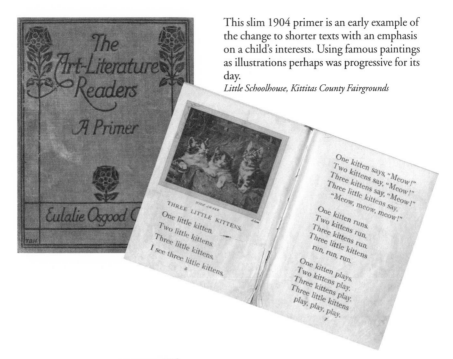

This slim 1904 primer is an early example of the change to shorter texts with an emphasis on a child's interests. Using famous paintings as illustrations perhaps was progressive for its day.
Little Schoolhouse, Kittitas County Fairgrounds

Color printing was common by 1928 when this reader appeared.
Little Schoolhouse, Kittitas County Fairgrounds

Elementary textbooks of the late 19th century generally served the dual purpose of teaching children to read while also inspiring them to lead proper and noble lives. Some books, such as the McGuffey Readers, combined syllabication and phonics with the sight word method to provide an effective teaching tool. These texts were popularly used right into the 20th century.

Many of the other readers used in the early 1900s, however, focused more on the sight word method, such as the Elson Readers, Sanders Series, Beacon Readers, and the Barnes Readers. On the other hand, the Gordon Readers were as effective as the earlier McGuffey in combining solid phonics instruction with interesting stories and sight words. One of the teachers in *Making the Grade* specifically mentioned that she taught phonics. She probably combined the two methods along with others, as sensible teachers have been doing all along no matter which basic text they had.

After the turn of the century, many newly published schoolbooks became more oriented to a child's point of view. This was especially reflected in the content and type of illustrations included in readers, geographies, and histories. Publishers' techniques for the use of color and photography were well laid down as the new century progressed into the 1910s and beyond, allowing the inclusion of improved lighter tone images and eventually adding photographs, which replaced the formerly dark and rather uninviting black and white illustrations of older textbooks. Color illustration went from single color tinted pictures, to two- and three-color tints, and eventually to full color by the 1930s.

Some early spellers, such as *The Descriptive Speller for Graded and Ungraded Schools* (1901), were specifically meant for use by a wide range of students in different grades as was typical in one room schools. These texts contained spelling lists and exercises for the third through eighth grades, allowing a child to review what they had learned in the past and to see what future study held in store, promoting an independent learning style. Spelling contests were extremely popular in the early 20th century. The American Book Company, publisher of the *Champion Spelling Book, Part One* for Grades 1–4 and *Part Two* for Grades 5–8 (1909), boasted that the students who had used their texts won many spelling competitions.

In the mid 1930s, these older, inclusive, hardbound volumes containing both pre-primer and primer reading lessons were replaced by shorter length, brightly colored, soft-back texts of 20, 40, or 50 pages with as much space dedicated to pictures as words. For a student reading to the

Run

Run, Tom, run.
Run, Jip, run.
Father is coming.

3

Illustrations in the *Webster Readers: Tom, Jip and Jane* (1932) were produced in extensive color—blues, yellows, and reds.
Little Schoolhouse, Kittitas County Fairgrounds

end of these very short books, it meant success for them, fostering an "I can read!" confidence. (As a retired first grade teacher, I can testify to the value of the short pre-primer. I have seen the glow on a child's face when she finished "a whole book" of 20 pages.)

Some arithmetic books had similar grade combination formats, but with narrower grade level groupings, such as the *Stone-Mills Arithmetic* publications dating from the 1910s and 1920s with texts for grades 1–4, 5–6, and 7–8. Educational methods sometimes swung in fads from one style to another and, by the late 1800s, "mental arithmetic" and drills had been adopted. "Mental arithmetic" introduced the concept of number manipulations by using oral questions and answers based on tangible objects already familiar to the students. This new theory, based on "understanding" as being the best path to learning arithmetic, questioned the memorization method in use since the 1600s.

In 1873, Edward Brooks had applied this method to classroom instruction in *The New Normal Mental Arithmetic*. The student was led though oral exercises revealing the sequential relationships between numbers, from which he or she could then recognize the underlying rules. In "mental arithmetic,"

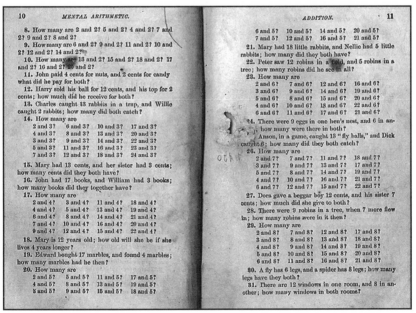

Edward Brooks, *The New Normal Mental Arithmetic: A Thorough and Complete Course by Analysis and Induction* (Philadelphia: Sower, Potts, 1873).
CWU Special Collections

ordinary words such as "and" or "how many?" were used instead of "+" and "=" signs for the first four lessons. Lesson 5 finally introduced the symbols for plus, minus, etc. Each new concept—multiplication, division, fractions, etc.—was introduced using familiar objects and ordinary language before tackling the mathematic symbols.

In the previous long-established method of rote memorization, the rules were given first and then written work, as drill, began in the first few lessons. Many instructors still preferred these older methods, however, which they termed "mental discipline" as opposed to Brooks' "mental arithmetic" model. In time, "mental arithmetic" was blended into "mental discipline," and the term "mental arithmetic" became synonymous with drill.

Geography texts of the 19th century often applied what modern commentators term the "shock and awe" appeal to young learners. Examples are shown here in illustrations from *Smith's First Book in Geography* (1848). Notice the dramatic lion and boa

Smith's First Book in Geography: An Introductory Geography Designed for Children (1848). *CWU Special Collections*

illustrations—these are included as attention-getting scenes, with effectively no explanation. But they provided children with supposed (but erroneous) representative views of life in Africa—i.e., the lion's daily fare is a Hottentot native, and boa constrictors are slavering creatures that boldly attack humans. Also note the disparaging remark above the picture of the lion carrying off a native: "The people are…destitute of intelligence." All this, of course, reflects prevailing social views and attitudes of the times, as do the "God-centered" facts from the same book:

Lesson 1—
Q: Who made the world?
A: God, the Maker of All Things.
Q: For what purpose did he make it?
A: To be a dwelling place of man.[15]

By the early 1900s, movement was afoot to provide accuracy and better understanding regarding other people and places around the globe. Geography texts were the first to embrace the new printing technologies by producing colored maps and illustrations, as well as good quality black and white images. The conversational travelogue style, relating a child's life in different geographical regions, was a popular method for teaching students about people and places—a good example being *Elementary Geography*, published by the Macmillan Company in 1921. *A Picture Book of Children around the World* (1934), a large 9" x 12" paperback, contains about two-dozen full pages of black and white pictures of children in cultural dress, with several lines of explanatory text below each photo. (I personally remember this volume from my own schoolgirl days in the early 1940s; good books stay around a classroom for a long time.)

History books followed a similar evolution in becoming more child-oriented. The earlier pattern of rote learning of dates, events, and facts gave way to a narrative approach as a means of engaging a young student's interest, such as *A History of the United States for Grammar Schools*, published by Houghton-Mifflin in 1924. The Progressive Movement even birthed a volume published by Charles Scribner's Sons, *Socialized History of the United States* (1931). It portrayed history in a people-focused manner, as opposed to the traditional event-centered format. Each section began with the inquiry, "How…"—i.e., "How the United States Is Peopled," "How Our Home Life Has Changed since Colonial Times," etc.

Special emphasis was put on health and hygiene in the 1920s. Students were graded for it on their report cards, and the Washington State examination taken by eighth graders asked them to identify parts of the body, muscles, etc. Two extensively used elementary hygiene books, one for grades 3–6 and another for 7–8, were published by the Lippincott Company in the *Modern Physiology Hygiene and Health* series in the early 1920s. The first book focused on personal health, while the second was more detailed and stressed the fact that good health would help a young person get a good job and make more money.

Regarding musical instruction, the Silver Burdett firm published *The Common School Book of Vocal Music: The Modern Music Series* (1904) in an ungraded format intended for one room schools. Older students used the book and taught the younger pupils. The authors felt there were advantages in a mixed grades approach to musical learning.

As some of the teachers note in *Making the Grade*, children coming from homes where newspapers and magazines were available generally did better

in school. A popular children's magazine, *Chatterbox*, was printed weekly in England, and imported to America in an "annual" format from 1878 until the 1950s. These large, well-illustrated volumes of several hundred pages contained numerous short stories, biographies, serial narratives, poems, puzzles, and vignettes with high moral tone that appealed to youngsters of many ages. The Ellensburg Public Library has a half dozen well thumbed examples dating from 1897 to 1903—these volumes undoubtedly were much loved and used for many years after their publication dates.

Ellensburg Public Library

A typical reading game from earlier times was *Peter Coddle's Trip to New York and What He Saw There: A Comical*

Combination of Curious Circumstances for 100 Evenings. It probably was mostly played at home. In the game, a player reads a short story until coming to a blank space; at this point, a card is randomly drawn from a pile to fill in the blank. When the short text on the card is read, it often results in a humorous, perhaps even ridiculous, addition to the story. Though copyrighted in 1882, this early version of "Mad Libs" probably was played into the early decades of the 20th century.[16] It was a fun way for children to fill up long dark evenings at home, while it also peripherally reinforced reading skills.[17]

Notes

1. A.J. Splawn, *Ka-mi-akin: The Last Hero of the Yakimas*, 160. Posthumously published in 1917, Splawn's book is one of the best historical accounts depicting pioneer times in central Washington.
2. In 1939, MAY SPURLING JANKOWSKI (see page 143) at the Upper Naneum School taught children from the John and Ida Nason household, an Indian family much respected in the local community.
3. Olmstead-Smith Collection, Miscellaneous Photographs, Washington State Archives, Central Regional Branch, Series CE952-21.
4. Local historian Leta May Smith gathered information from old-timers' reminiscences, letters, scrapbooks, report cards, and scribbles in old textbooks and on scraps of paper to piece together a partial, though valuable, overview of the early schools. See Leta May Smith, *The End of the Trail* (Hicksville, New York: Exposition Press, 1976).
5. According to the modern-day Consumer Price Index, $10 in 1877 would be equivalent to $192.41 in 2005. Information provided courtesy of Milton Wagy, Local History Librarian, Ellensburg Public Library.
6. Records are scanty in regard to the newly planned school in 1889.
7. "The winding switch back...was a terror to most of those who ever crossed it. The general fear and discomfort and car sickness of a crossing was described by one who had been over it: '...first you are lying on your back and the next minute you are on the floor.'" Leta May Smith, *The End of the Trail* (1976), 270.
8. *Ellensburgh Capitol*, June 20, 1889, quoted in Samuel R. Mohler, "Boom Days in Ellensburg, 1888–1891," *Pacific Northwest Quarterly*, Vol. 36, No. 4 (October 24, 1945), 291.
9. Mohler, cited above, provides a readable in-depth study of Ellensburg's "boom and bust" years.
10. The authors of *An Illustrated History of Klickitat, Yakima and Kittitas Counties* (1904, p. 268) stated: "It has always been characteristic of the American Republic that it emerges from a foreign war stronger, more vigorous, more wealthy, more prosperous than at the beginning of hostilities."

11. For the "State of Washington Teachers' Examinations," see Appendix B in *Making the Grade*.
12. Washington State Normal School, *Quarterly Catalogs*, 1892–1921. In these years, the state legislature and the faculty frequently introduced new variations in admission standards, certificate designations, and graduation/diploma requirements with many references in the course catalogs to "or equivalent," "exceptions," and other modifications. For additional information, see Samuel R. Mohler, *The First Seventy-Five Years: A History of Central Washington State College, 1891–1966* (Ellensburg: Central Washington State College, 1967).
13. Edith McMurry Ellexson in, Centennial Committee of Central Washington University, *Central Remembered: A Collection of Memories and Anecdotes* (Ellensburg: CWU Auxiliary Services, 1992).
14. Today, the modern Damman School on the Manastash Road near Ellensburg is the one remaining rural school in Kittitas County.
15. Roswell Chamberlain Smith, *Smith's First Book in Geography: An Introductory Geography Designed for Children*, 8th edition (Portland, Maine: Sanborne and Carter, 1848), 9.
16. Peter Coddle's Trip to New York is archived in CWU Special Collections. Today's modern "Mad Libs" books (and card games) typically have a short story on each page, with blank spaces for adding key words. Under each blank space, a specified type of word is called for, such as a noun, verb, etc. A player, without revealing the story, asks other participants in turn to contribute words for each of the blanks. Then, when the story is read out loud, it usually results in a humorous narration.
17. For an additional example of a book game played by children, see *The Electrical Wonder Book* in Appendix D.

1

Sharpen Up Your Six-Shooter

Elsie Hodgson Schnebly, 1914–17

Elsie's story is compiled from three sources: a recorded oral interview, a tape of her talk to the Kittitas County Historical Museum, and a typed memoir she created for her family, which was loaned to me by her son, Frank Schnebly Jr.

It was 1914. I was 18. I had one year at Ellensburg Normal, but no experience. In those days if you had two years of high school and a year at Normal you could take an examination to teach. I was able to pass it and also music and get above 90. I received a certificate allowing me to teach for two years. To gain experience, the superintendent said I must apply to some of the little schools in the hills, where an older teacher would be unable to do the work.

Well, there were more teachers than schools at that time and it looked like I'd be lucky to get anything at all. I could've taught at my home school—my mother was the clerk and the directors were friends—but I knew it would be a poor thing for me to start teaching there with all the neighbors criticizing.

And so I sent my timid applications out and waited. Day followed day. At last on August 16, 1914, I saw my father coming from town waving a letter and a newspaper. The headlines said war had been declared in Europe, but I could hardly wait to read the letter. It was from Mr. Judkins, clerk of Tarpiscan School, District #19, on the Columbia River.

He wrote, "You can teach our school. We pay $60 per month. You can board with us for $20 a month, if you can stand 9 kids. Sharpen up your six-shooter, we got some ornery kids in these parts. School will start October 12, for 6 months. Let me know if you're coming and I'll get a contract made."

We all read the letter over and over. I thought it sounded fun and kind of exciting, but the part about the six-shooter made my mother hesitate. My parents talked to others. So many rumors: "The people over there had stills, made their own licker," and much more, but only partially true. I later found these people to be kind, hospitable, and honest, and they always treated me with respect and later with affection. I liked and enjoyed them all.

My mother finally said to take the offer and I sent my letter of acceptance at once. I can still remember working in the fields that day. The sun was bright and hot. Farmers were cutting their second crop of alfalfa, the air was sweet with the smell of

Elsie, age 11 or 12.
Frank Schnebly Jr.

new-cut hay, and I was happy to drive the horses on the hay rake so I could think without interruption. The meadowlarks sang and my heart sang with them. At last I would be a teacher.

The Tarpiscan School stood in the hills near the Columbia River. It was only 30 miles from my home in the Kittitas Valley, but the very poor road led over steep ridges and mountains. On the other hand, to get there by train, one had to go 200 miles east on the Northern Pacific to Spokane, change to the Great Northern, and then come back to the center of the state. Or, one could take the Milwaukee Road and by a round-about way get to the Columbia River and the school. So we wondered how I should go.

Then a telegram arrived on Wednesday. It said to take the Milwaukee at midnight on Wednesday from Ellensburg to Warden. Then on Thursday, take a train to Adrian and wait there until Saturday. Then take the Great Northern to Vulcan and someone would meet me there. I already had been packed for days, but still had things to do. "Be a good girl, don't do anything you would be ashamed to tell me and if anything worries you, write home." I guess you could call that my sex education or facts of life talk. At least that was the only advice I ever received, but it was enough. A girl who sees decency and honesty in the daily life of her own home develops an instinct for what is right or wrong.

When I boarded the train in Ellensburg at midnight everyone was drowsy or asleep, but I was wide awake and thrilled to be traveling at last. From my first day as a youngster in school, I wanted to be a teacher. I daydreamed about it. My happiest days were the ones when I heard the spelling class or the little ones recite. When it was my turn to choose what we played, we played school, especially singing. I stood up on an old tree stump as my sister pounded on an overturned wash tub, and we sang. "Tramp, tramp, tramp, the boys are marching" was especially good to sing, and also "Bringing in the Sheaves."

As I grew older, I worked for my room and board to go to school, which caused me to miss much of the fun in those years. But always before me was the dream—some day I would teach and all life's problems would be solved. At last here I was—through high school and Normal School, with my teaching certificate, and on my way to my first job. I was just full of questions. What kind of school was Tarpiscan? What would my boarding be like? What was in Vulcan?

The conductor tapped me on the shoulder. "You are going to Warden; will someone meet you?"

"No."

"Do you know where to go?"

"No."

"I'll be back."

Soon he returned. "There is a Mr. Brown on the train. He is a salesman for a hardware store. He is stopping at Warden. He will show you to the hotel."

So trustingly, after getting off in Warden, I followed Mr. Brown to the only hotel. I was to find that same kindness and assistance from almost everyone I met. Warden at the time consisted of a depot, hotel, store, and a few other small buildings.

At 10 a.m. on Thursday, my trunk and I were taken out by a team and wagon to where I stepped onto the funniest little train you ever saw. Besides the engine, it consisted of only a baggage car and a passenger coach. A half-dozen men and a young girl were on board. The girl was bored because she'd taken this train ride many times, but everyone else was out to entertain me and I laughed with them as we rode along. At every crossroad, the train stopped to pick up milk cans or a passenger. The engineer blew the whistle for every jackrabbit on the track, and he would tease the little rotund man loading the milk cans, making him run for the train. At noon we stopped at a one-store town for an hour where the men bought bananas, raisins, and crackers.

At one o'clock, we were off. Since the little train was the only one on the track, they set their own time. At two o'clock, we arrived in Adrian, where the train crew carried my baggage to the hotel, while the elderly conductor warned me to keep my door locked.

On Saturday, the Great Northern came puffing into the station—a "big city" train, with no smiles, no speaking to strangers, and all business. I missed the companionship of my friends on the funny little train. But I was on my way to Vulcan.

I got off in a pouring rain. Vulcan was only a post with a sign on it. There wasn't a house in sight, only sand dunes and sagebrush as far as I could see, with the Columbia River out of sight behind a rise. I sat on my trunk for two hours. Finally, a young man arrived, very bashful but nice. He was Sam Judkins and between us we carried my baggage to the river.

This was my first view of the Columbia—wide, quiet, with that deceptively slow appearance of deep water. Two young boys standing near a boat said they were going to take us across. I had my doubts, but they seemed so assured. They were Henry and Arthur Coffin, 13-year-old twin sons of Lester Coffin. They handled that boat as easily as town boys rode a bicycle.

I was to learn much more about the Columbia when teaching at Tarpiscan that year, and during the next year at the Sunset School farther along the river. It wasn't bravery but my ignorance that kept me from being afraid of the big river. For instance, that first winter the Columbia froze over so hard that men drove hay wagons across to feed cattle on the other side. On Saturdays, we girls sometimes went along for the ride. It didn't occur to me that the popping sounds might be from the ice cracking.

Then there was the time that some older girls wanted to go across the river to a dance and begged their mother for permission. She said (as other mothers also did on other occasions): "It will be alright only if teacher goes too and says it is safe."

An 18-year-old boy rowed us over. The ice was breaking up and huge chunks floated down. We sang and laughed as the boy rowed fast to miss an iceberg, then rowed back upstream as far as the current would allow and then proceeded ahead. Fate was kind to us, nothing happened, but I wasn't brave, just ignorant of danger.

When I crossed the Columbia that first time with the Coffin twins and Sam Judkins, I could see a low, ranch-type stone house with roses blooming in the yard. Standing adjacent to it were neat buildings and corrals. This was the Coffin family's home. It was full of Indian relics, with Navajo blankets on the walls, floors, and beds. A huge fireplace stretched across one end of the living room—big enough to burn a full round of a log. And there was a piano and lots of books. (The house later burned down and the Coffins replaced it with a bigger structure called "The Castle.") To me, the stone house was tasteful and just right for its mountain and river setting.

Mr. Coffin was a genial host and made me feel welcome, as did his wife, Grace. They owned large holdings in this mountainous area—just right for his herds of cattle and sheep. Their land adjoined the many acres belonging to Frank Rothrock and P.H. Schnebly, later called the Schnebly Brothers.

"Spanish Castle" in the Cape Horn area, with the Horn
Trail in the background.
Ellensburg Public Library

Construction of the Spanish Castle was completed in 1918 at a cost of more than
$20,000 by Lester Coffin, according to reports in the *Wenatchee Daily World*. Coffin
and his brother were Yakima-based cattlemen and "lords of the Tarpiscan range who
counted their horses, cattle and sheep by the thousands," according to a May 21, 1927,
World article.

Coffin dreamed for years of having a home along the Columbia River, resembling
the residence of a Mexican president of the early 1900s. The location he chose, on
the river at the mouth of Tarpiscan Creek, was two miles into Kittitas County from the
Kittitas-Chelan county line. It was remote and almost inaccessible.

An earlier rock house at the site had burned. Construction materials for the new
house were hauled over the rough Colockum Pass Road in covered wagons. Some materials were brought in from across the river. The house had 13 to 17 rooms, including
a spacious entrance hall, reception room, living room, five bedrooms, two bathrooms,
and an indoor pool.

Coffin didn't get to enjoy it. Just a few days after it was done, he died in a Wenatchee
hospital. The Spanish Castle had several other owners before it was bought and torn
down by the Grant County PUD in 1963 to make way for the Wanapum Dam reservoir.
—*Colin Condit*

The three large holdings provided work for many of the young men from the
canyons and meadowlands. I didn't know it then, but the livestock business
would become my way of life after my marriage. At this time, teaching school
seemed the most interesting occupation to me.

Mr. Coffin, who was wheelchair bound, told me a little about the cowboys, a fascinating subject, as well as the local social life, mostly the weekly
dances. He pointed to a big bluff above his home and a trail leading around

it. In places, the bluff hung above the river and traveling that way was called going "around the Horn." He said, "Some day you'll be riding around that trail."

I looked at the sheer drop and the swirling water below, and thought, "Never." I then said, "I can't even ride a horse."

"Those cowboys will teach you," he said. They did, but that came later.

Sam had the horses ready and I climbed into the wagon and we were off, over a rocky road up Tarpiscan Canyon. The sun was low and, after the rain, the air chilly. Shrubs were turning color after the early frost; their gold, red, and orange foliage against the green trees made for a beautiful contrast. I was thinking what a lovely country it was.

"Whoa," Sam stopped the team. "There's your schoolhouse."

My first look was a shock. It was a little unpainted building, with wooden shutters over the windows, some broken. Woodpeckers had drilled holes all along the walls and tall weeds covered the grounds. Two little outhouses with sagging doors stood in back.

"Oh, can we stop a bit so I can see inside?" I jumped down and began to run through the weeds.

"Look out for snakes," Sam called out, "because we sure got lots of them."

Snakes, the thing I feared most. I tried the door. It was locked, but through the window I could see lots of yellow jackets, dead flies, and dust.

We drove on. Darkness settled gradually as we rode through the big orchard on the Campbell place. I was cold and hungry, and a little depressed at seeing the schoolhouse. I was wondering where I'd board. We stopped at the Judkins. They were people from Tennessee and a lot different than anybody I'd ever known, but they were wonderful to me—kind and good people, but quite poverty stricken. We arrived at dark. The door opened and Mr. Judkins stepped out with a kerosene lamp and Mrs. Judkins with a baby, and their boys and girls kept coming out too. They had nine children—Daisy, Jessie, Charlie, Maggie, Dick, Dyke, Louise, Sam, and Tom.

"Howdy, Miss Elsie," he said. "Get down and set."

As I stepped down, I was as excited in meeting them as they were in seeing me. Willing hands carried my baggage into the warm house. A table was set for dinner in the large living-dining room. All the little ones escorted me upstairs, which was divided into two large bedrooms—one for the girls (and me) and one for the boys. Our girls' room contained three double beds. I was given the bed in the corner; with my trunk beside me, it became my "room." It was a large, high bed, with an extra thick feather mattress. I was to find this the most comfortable and warmest bed I ever slept in. But I never mastered the art of making the bed properly. It always sagged where I'd slept. There was a way of using a broom handle to level it off.

When going downstairs, everyone was hungry, but an argument started among the children as to who would sit by "teacher." I settled it by taking a place between the two littlest ones, and that became their reward throughout the winter. If they were good, they could sit by "teacher." No one could be socially stiff after this; they took me into their lives wholeheartedly and I was very fond of them.

The Judkins were real good to me. They treated me just like a daughter. Every night, we had a square dance as Mr. Judkins played the fiddle and his children picked on the banjo. Eventually, I brought back geography books from the school; that's the only library they had. I read out loud to the children about an hour every evening, and they just seemed to absorb it. They were so hungry for learning. I'd had two years of German at school. Every German word I could teach them they just seemed to take in.

The children were clean and well behaved, and I almost never heard them quarrel or get a scolding. Mrs. Judkins had a unique way of letting them learn by experience. I came home one evening and little Dyke, perhaps 18 months old, was walking around in his usual unsteady baby walk, carrying a big butcher knife. I ran to take the knife away, but Mrs. Judkins said, "Leave him be. He's always wanting that knife. If he gets hurt it will teach him to leave it alone." I hurried upstairs and shut the door so I couldn't hear him crying if he got hurt, but nothing happened.

At that first meal we had a feast—chicken and dumplings, hot beaten soda biscuits with honey, and sauerkraut. They were pleased that I liked sauerkraut and showed me the 50 gallon barrel in which they made it. They cut the cabbage fine, but every so often cored a whole cabbage and threw it into the barrel, to be chopped up with a clean spade. When eating it, one often took in a big chunk, but it was the best flavored kraut I ever tasted.

As the winter wore on our menu narrowed. The cow went dry, so there was no milk, butter, or cream. Then we ate the last of the pork. As the weather grew colder, the hens quit laying. The sauerkraut barrel was empty. Toward spring, our menu consisted of boiled white beans, biscuits with water gravy, prunes, pears, and apples.

Of apples we had plenty, all of the Ben Davis variety. If any one remembers them, they are dry and tasteless, but wonderful keepers. The fall before, the whole family had worked hard to pick and pack hundreds of boxes of Ben Davis apples for selling, but then there was no market. Disappointed, the family dug a big pit, dumped in the apples, and covered them with clean straw and then piles of dirt. The apples kept perfectly. This same method was used to store potatoes, carrots, and cabbage.

Their large orchard had numerous pear trees and the crop had been good. The pears were picked, boxed, and shipped east to market. Eagerly they awaited the check and talked about their spending plans. Bills were outstanding, especially $400 for the funeral of Mr. Judkins' mother. But this was 1914, and there was a depression. They talked openly of their worries, and I was concerned with them.

Finally a letter arrived; a billing for $8 dropped out. The pears had been sold, but brought too little cash to pay for the freight. I thought that just wasn't fair—some of their socialistic views seemed to make more sense to me then. Today, many of the economic and workplace reforms that the Judkins had hoped for are taken for granted as common sense measures and are not thought of as socialistic.

The day after I arrived at the Judkins, I was anxious to get started and left at daylight to walk the mile or more to the school to clean it up. The room was full of dead flies and yellow jackets, and an old organ in the corner had a mouse nest in it. I cleaned up the organ and got a little tune out of it, but there was no sheet music. After cleaning the room, I looked around to see what I had to work with. There were a few pieces of chalk about an inch long, but no ink, pencils, tablets, or color crayons. I did find a few old schoolbooks, as well as 20 dusty geography/travel books that some past director had probably been criticized for wasting money on. I silently blessed him for these books, and also was thankful for the volumes in my little trunk, which had made it so heavy to move. Those old geography books and my half trunk of books were my only help.

When I returned to the house, I told Mr. Judkins what I needed. He replied, "Well, I'm a socialist. If you want any of that fancy stuff, you'll have to buy it yourself. The district has just enough to pay your salary for 6 months." They did have a Sears, Roebuck catalog, so I made out a big order that night.

The next day I went down to the school to see how many students I'd have. I had eight pupils; six from the Judkins family and the two Coffin boys—that was all. The Coffin boys were good students, but full of mischief, though all the children were good and I loved them all.

Before the first day of school, Mr. Judkins said, "I'm a socialist and I don't want my children saying the allegiance to the flag."

My ritual book, however, said to expel any student who wouldn't recite the oath of allegiance, but that would be six of my children. I couldn't afford to do without them and they needed schooling, so I told them they could just sit in their seats while the two Coffin boys recited it.

On the first Friday, Mr. Judkins came over to the school and heard the Coffin boys give the oath of allegiance. He said, "Why didn't my children speak that piece?"

When I told him, he replied, "Oh, is that the oath of allegiance?" He didn't know what it was, but he'd heard it wasn't a socialist thing.

One afternoon, a young man came to the school with a rifle under one arm and a bible under the other. He wanted to learn to be a preacher. I said, "Well, you start reading."

He opened the bible at Genesis and with difficulty mouthed the words, "In…the…"

I said, "Beginning."

He said, "Beginning…"

That's the way it went from the first. He came for part of three days and then quit. I tried to instruct him, but he just couldn't learn and I was frightened of him. Poor fella, that was all the schooling he had.

The students had a lot of catching up to do. They were bright enough, but in the previous short school terms they'd been unable to complete the full year's work. I faced a dilemma. If we reviewed and tried to catch up on what they'd missed the previous year, that would leave too little time to do even six months work in their present courses. It was unfair to the pupils and to me, but we tried.

With students in almost all eight grades, a tight schedule had to be maintained. Sometimes I'd combine two spelling classes. Often, the older students

The six Judkins students at the Tarpiscan School; note the woodpecker holes in the wall and shutter. *Frank Schnebly Jr.*

listened to the little ones read, while I helped others with arithmetic. We also combined geography classes. The little ones learned from observing the older students. The children who read books, newspapers, and magazines at home were much better informed and understood the lessons more easily.

While I instructed the children, the local people told me about rattle-snakes. The directors gave me a quart of whiskey to keep on hand in case a child was bitten, but none were. Lots of harmless blue racer snakes were just as frightening to me. In the spring, hogs were turned out to root in the sage-brush. They killed the snakes and never seemed to suffer from bites.

One day, Mr. Coffin, who was paralyzed from the waist down and in a wheelchair, came up to the school. A Japanese man took care of him and helped him travel in a kind of little wagon. They brought the Coffins' pet monkey with them. When they came into the school, right away it jumped up on a window sill and grabbed a bottle of ink and tried to drink it. This upset the whole school, but it was fun.

Though there were only eight students, on the Friday before Christmas we put on a holiday program with carols and recitations. I'd made little mos-quito netting bags, putting in each an orange, some nuts, and a little hard candy to pass out after the program. Word about the event got around. Six-teen miles north in Colockum Canyon, there were lots of orchards where hired men picked and packed fruit. In the winter, these men, who were holed up in one room shacks, had lots of spare time and energy. Hearing about the school program, they borrowed horses and came on over. With these men, plus the mothers and other people arriving, we didn't have enough chairs, so they brought in blocks of wood to sit on.

They joined in singing, and everything went along fine until I passed out the treat and candy bags. I didn't have enough for all the men. When one of them stuck a bag in his pocket and the others saw him do it, they started yell-ing and invited him outside to the biggest fight you ever saw. I was just sick! I thought, "There goes my good school program."

But Mrs. Judkins said, "Just pay no never mind. They've been dying for a fight. They've been penned up so long. All that muscle and nothing to do. It will do them good."

They rolled in the snow and had a good fight. The next night at the dance, there were a lot of black eyes and skinned faces. They all looked kind of sheepish, but seemed pretty happy. I guess they really enjoyed it.

Each week in this country, talk focused on the Saturday night dances, which were held in packing sheds over on the Colockum. With all the fruit pickers and cowboys attending, there were about five men to each girl. Of course, the only social recreation available was the dances. So everybody wanted to go.

In those days, there were no cars out in this country and almost no roads. We had to go by horseback to the dances, but I didn't know how to ride nor did I own a riding skirt. Out came the Sears, Roebuck catalog with beautiful pictures of long divided skirts, which flapped in the wind as one rode. A selection for a skirt was included with the order for crayons and chalk.

When my first Saturday dance came up, the skirt hadn't arrived, but we all wanted to go. I loved to dance and I could drive a team of horses. The Judkins said, "You mean you can drive two horses hitched together?"

Raised on a farm, I answered, "Of course, can't everyone?"

Dubiously, they discussed the possibility, and the danger, of allowing me to drive with the two older girls. The thoughts of the dance won out, however.

The team proved to be two small Cayuses, the kind my brother called "jackrabbit" size. They were skittish and the buggy was old. I held their heads until we were ready to start. Then I held the lines firmly and with a dash and a scream from the girls we were off at a gallop. I didn't understand how girls who'd ride any kind of horse could be afraid of two hitched together. And they didn't understand how I could be so ignorant about a riding horse. They had many a laugh at my expense.

When my skirt arrived, I had to learn to ride first thing. I said, "If you get a real gentle one, I'll learn to ride."

They talked it over, and thought I could ride Nellie. All the kids tittered, "Old Nellie!" Then they brought her out—an old white horse, the color they called "flea-bitten." Her eyes were half shut and her head hung almost to the ground. She had a broad sagging stomach and big flat feet.

I said, "Show me how to get on." The kids were tickled to teach me something—how to get on, how to hold the reins.

She was saddled up, and I tried to get on. "Not that side, the other one." "Hold the reins in one hand."

With a boost I was up. My toes pointed out over the horse's fat belly. I tried to pull up her head; no luck. Then I thought I'd walk her. I clucked and pushed on the reins, with everyone laughing. She just stood there with that sad look. I clucked and kicked and she wouldn't start. The other horses began to rear up and get excited. Finally, when they started on, all of a sudden old "flea-bitten" raised her head and followed. I found out she was the Coffin's old packhorse, the one they used to carry supplies out to the sheep camps. She'd been trained to follow other horses and that's the way I rode her, always behind the others.

Her gait was a steady "plop, plop," no gallop, no pace, no walk—just "plop, plop, plop, plop" went those big flat feet for 16 miles. I learned that to survive this I'd have to sit light. I suppose I learned it, because two years later when I rode with my husband-to-be, Frank Schnebly, he admired the way I rode. His greatest compliment, one that I'd learned the hard way, was "You sit a horse like a man." I rode 16 miles to dances on that horse. Danced all night and rode back the next day.

After a few weeks, "flea-bitten" returned to her normal occupation of packing supplies and I was presented with an even sadder looking horse. For want of a better name, I shall call her "knock-knock," because she was so knock-kneed in front. After a few yards of galloping, her poor knees locked up, and then down on her knees she'd go, but always with plenty of time for me to step out of the stirrups. She then would rise up, give herself a shake, and on we went.

The women rode to the dances with dresses tied on behind the saddles. Getting chaperones was no problem, as we all rode together in groups, picking up riders along the way. We also rode home in groups, but there was no stopping or dallying on horseback when the temperature sunk below zero.

At the dances, they had a fiddle and an organ to back it up, and sometimes a banjo. You'd never dance with a man who had anything to drink; in those days drinking wasn't considered very good. The first one who asked you for the supper dance was considered your date. You'd have two or three dances promised to him, but there were no programs. No one ever just asked you; they'd always get somebody to introduce you to them—that was part of the social life.

They all seemed to be a happy group. Babies were brought along and sometimes left sleeping under a bench or on a pile of coats. Wheat ranchers from Quincy flats and the cowboys might fight outside, but that didn't bother the dancers inside the packing shed.

Teachers were always popular. There was a shortage of women out in these rural areas and plenty of bachelors wanting wives. A lot of men came to the dances, and a teacher had a really good time. You'd get some proposals and all that, but it was just because of the female shortage. Most teachers eventually did marry somebody in their district. The Ladies Aid group presented each bride with a quilt that the group made. Some of them would come around to single women, slyly asking if you wanted a quilt sewn.

No one was ever turned away at meal time. Mrs. Ingersoll or others cooked a big supper for $1 per couple served at midnight. Then we danced until 4 a.m. After the dance, someone would ask us to breakfast. Men shot the heads off some chickens and skinned them—inside of an hour, fried chicken, hot biscuits, gravy, and coffee would be ready for us before the long ride home.

There were many visitors to the Colockum—traveling musicians, hawkers, and politicians who were mostly socialists. A few worried that I might be a spy since I was surely a capitalist by earning all of $60 a month, whereas Mr. Judkins received $60 for feeding cattle and had nine children to feed. However, I was sympathetic, ever since the episode with the pear shipment that sold too little to even pay all the freight charges.

Often on Fridays, the Coffin boys came leading an extra horse and an invitation for me to spend the weekend with their housekeeper, Ruby Mettler, a young teacher unable to find a school that year. We spent many happy days together—reading, playing piano, talking, and laughing at the boys' pranks. Mr. and Mrs. Coffin had gone to California for the winter, so Miss Mettler was more of a companion to the twins rather than just being a housekeeper.

One of the boys' pranks was to bring their pet monkey into the room. It was the first monkey I'd been around. I was afraid, yet fascinated by its antics. I liked to watch it eat. One time when visitors were present, the monkey was given hot cakes to eat. It would hold a pancake in its little hands, taking small bites all around the edge. All the while, those little black eyes darted all around. One of the older women laughed so hard that her upper denture fell out. Quick as a flash, the monkey dropped its pancake and dived for the teeth, only to bump heads with the woman who luckily grasped her denture first.

The monkey first reached out for something with its front arms, then whirled around and reached it with its longer hind legs. The monkey caused a lot of commotion and fun, but it came to a sad end. One cold day it got loose outside and climbed a tall pole. The men called and coaxed, but it stayed up there long enough to become thoroughly chilled, later developing pneumonia. The boys doctored the poor monkey, but it finally died, making us all sad. The boys prepared it for burial, and played "Custer's Funeral March" on the phonograph.

One Monday morning, when we were ready to go to the school, a beautiful black horse was led up for me to ride. Named Black Diamond, it was Mrs. Coffin's own saddle horse. I think that was the day I fell in love with horses. Black Diamond was all that a well-bred horse should be—small and dainty feet, head held high with bright alert eyes, coat shiny black, and a gait that was something to dream about, so swift, so smooth. The few times I was fortunate enough to ride this beautiful black horse stand out in my memory.

I was the last instructor to teach at the Tarpiscan School. The following year, the Judkins children were taught at home by Ina Dewees, and the Coffin boys moved to Seattle.

Elsie (on horseback, second from right) with the Rothrocks in front of their home in the Brushy, 1915.
Frank Schnebly Jr.

I next taught at the Sunset School in the Brushy, south of the Tarpiscan area. There were all kinds of people in the Brushy Creek locality—a retired army major, cattlemen, sheep men, and real poverty stricken people. The Sunset District had telephone service, which was only a line strung on fence posts, but it was a great help. Each morning at eight o'clock, callers compared the outside temperatures. It always was two degrees colder nearer the river. I had 17 students and they all rode horseback to school, except for the children from the Rothrock home, where I boarded. The three Rothrock children lived close enough to walk.

A big wood stove heated the schoolhouse. One day, my clerk brought down a load of logs and dumped them on the school grounds. He said I could have the children split it up for me. Well, we knew about green logs, and we couldn't do anything with an old dull axe. So I excused them, saying we'd stay home until we got some decent wood. The next day the clerk and his two grown sons came and split it all up for us. Part of the recess activities each day included hauling in firewood.

Late each afternoon, I arranged kindling and wood for the following morning. This was the winter of 1915–16, the year of big snow. Each morning I had to walk almost two miles to the school. Those were the days when women wore hobble skirts. Imagine wearing a hobble skirt in deep snow!

Fortunately, there wasn't a house in sight after I passed the family orchard. I'd pull up my skirt so I could get through the drifts to the schoolhouse. I then started a fire to warm up the room before the children arrived.

It was an awfully cold winter, down to 4 or 6 below zero much of the time. The six Osborn children rode four miles to school on a pair of horses. They often were so cold that I'd carry them inside and rub their feet to thaw them out. Then we'd play marching games to get their circulation going. About an hour later, the chilblains would start to itch; those poor kids scratched their feet, and the little ones cried. It got to the point that each day began with the children marching around and around the stove while I played the old organ as loud as I could. They all sang. The cold was quite hard on them, but we managed nevertheless.

I had one disciplinary problem. Most children were quite good, but one boy kept doing little things all the time. He was from a family of 12 kids; he'd turn their horses loose so they had to walk home, or sometimes we'd have to run and catch the horses. He'd also tie up the gate so the children couldn't get their horses out; just little things like that. Finally I just had to paddle him.

His mother had a habit of writing notes to me every day, so I expected to hear from her. Mostly she praised me for having spelling matches and such, which was great. But this time—this boy's only 12 years old and I just wore out the switch on him—I felt bad too. Anyway, I received a note next morning and she said it was about time I did something. They couldn't do anything with him at home.

That poor boy, all he wanted was attention; he had 11 brothers and sisters. After learning that, I let him help clean the erasers and put out the chalk, and then he was the best little boy. After he grew up, he come by and said, "You're the only teacher ever learned me anything."

That's the only time I had to apply discipline. I knew he just wanted attention, because he was just so crowded out. But most of the children were real good and I just loved every one of them. It was a lot of fun; I loved teaching and liked the way the parents always cooperated. Teacher's word was good and most parents supported you in everything.

That year we held our school picnic on sand dunes along the Columbia. We'd climb up on those big sand hills, sit down, put out our feet, and slide down. The older girls and I, wearing riding skirts, sat with each grasping the feet of the one behind and then coasted down; it was fun.

When I taught at the Sunset School, we attended dances at Trinidad, crossing the river on Henry Davies' ferry. In the winter we stayed overnight at the hotel until daylight, or stayed later if ice interfered with the ferry.

Sunset School, 1908–25.
Ellensburg Public Library

Sometimes we rode our horses on the famous Horn Trail that Mr. Coffin had pointed out to me the year before. He'd told me then that one day I'd ride along that precarious route, and I remembered thinking, "Never!" But there I was, riding along, but we did lead our horses in places where the trail was just shale and not really a trail at all, above a sheer drop to a whirlpool in the river.

There were two horses I grew to love for their strength, courage, and faithfulness. They belonged to Cort Rothrock, who ran a big livestock operation and in whose home I boarded when teaching at the Sunset School. When Thanksgiving vacation approached that year, I was anxious to visit my parents. It was 30 miles over the pass to my home. For my trip on horseback, Mr. Rothrock chose a big, strong, older horse and was emphatic with this advice, "If it should snow, don't try to guide your horse, just give her her head and she'll bring you home."

I reached home with no difficulty. After a satisfying visit and a big Thanksgiving dinner, my parents began to worry about my return trip. Heavy clouds hung over the valley, and a look toward the mountains showed they were completely hidden in a dark, stormy mist on top. I started out on Sunday morning, and after just a few miles it began to snow. The horse was too big to run, but how she could walk! We went mile after mile, and snow fell faster as we climbed higher. When finally reaching the summit, the wind was so strong that it blew snow straight at me. I covered my nose with a kerchief against the cold as the cowboys had taught me.

As the snow grew heavier, I felt completely lost. The trees on all sides looked alike, with no familiar landmarks. I was sure we were going in the wrong direction. The horse held her head into the wind and kept up that fast steady walk. Over and over I repeated Mr. Rothrock's advice: Give her "her head," don't try to guide her. Hour after hour we continued; it grew dark and still we kept on. All of a sudden, the horse stopped! There stood Mr. and Mrs. Rothrock opening the gate with a lighted lantern held high. I slid off, stiff and cold, to be hugged by Mrs. Rothrock, while her husband took that wonderful old horse to the barn.

As Christmas vacation grew near, the question again arose about going home, but would the snow be too deep? Then a letter arrived from the Rothrock's daughter, Mabel, who attended high school in Ellensburg at the time. She planned to come to the edge of the mountains with my brother, meet me there, and then ride my horse back to the Rothrock ranch, while I would ride on toward Ellensburg with my brother. It sounded simple; only it kept snowing. With no telephone service there was no way to tell if Mabel was coming or not.

Mr. Rothrock finally planned it out. We started out on two strong horses and drove four big work horses ahead of us to break trail. The snow was too deep for the horses to walk; they jumped or lunged each step of the way. On the summit, snowdrifts reached the lower branches of trees. We went around as many drifts as we could and broke through the others. After many hours and with very tired horses, we came down into the valley. No one was there to meet us! When we reached the nearest telephone, we found out that Mabel thought we wouldn't come because of the deep snow. She went home by train. I continued on to my home, while Mr. Rothrock went back through the deep snow in the mountains. I was forced to leave my horse in the valley until spring and returned to the Rothrocks by train.

The other horse I loved was named Jim—a big, beautiful, dappled gray saddle horse with a gait we called a single foot. I rode him many times over the mountains, singing all the way. The horse seemed to keep time as I sang, or perhaps I timed my songs to his gait.

We sang a lot in those days. At the Judkins, some played the banjo or harmonica, and the Rothrocks had a piano. Every Sunday evening, we sang until the wee hours—all the old hymns, or old songs like "By the Light of the Silvery Moon" or "Meet Me Tonight in Dreamland." We sang loud and hearty, and we enjoyed it. One old gentleman always had me play "Where the River Shannon Flows" as it reminded him of his daughter.

The third year, 1916–17, I taught at Fairview, which was a nine month school located in the Kittitas Valley and much closer to my parents home. It paid $75 a month and the school was more up to date, with a better organ and more supplies, but I only had four students. When my future husband had been a youngster at Fairview School some time earlier, there were 30, 40, or 50 students for a few years, when the sessions included three months in the fall and three months in springtime. Some of the students were 21 years old before they got through, but that was before my time. The oldest student I had was 16 and in the seventh grade.

Fairview School, District #4, spring 1918.
Ellensburg Public Library

There was a sort of social center at Fairview called Youngman Hall where dances were held. Of course, in this community we went home right after the dances. But over on the Columbia where we rode horseback, we'd have breakfast before starting home. I don't know how the women did it; they must've worked hard while the rest of us sat around dozing off until breakfast was served.

Supervisors didn't visit me over on the Columbia; it was too far away for them to travel there. But at Fairview, a superintendent came several times. She had to send in reports on me and other teachers. (When I was a child in school, I remember one male superintendent who dozed off, sleeping through part of his observation time.) No questions were asked about the curriculum; it was taken for granted that an instructor taught what they were supposed to. I never was asked about the books that I assigned, or anything like that.

The districts I taught in were so poor that we just had the books we could scramble up. We weren't always up to date. Whatever I could find and whatever I took with me was what we had. I felt that the students who did well were the ones having magazines, books, and music in their home life. They were prepared to grasp new subjects and to study.

The school districts were supported by taxes on the people who resided there. The poorer districts had shorter school terms and paid less salary. My wages in the first year were $360 for six months, and that was all they'd set aside. When that was gone, we quit. During my second year, they provided transportation money for any child that lived over two miles from school.

One family received $40 a month for the use of two old horses, so the district ran out of money after six months and we closed the school. Although my contract called for working nine months, I didn't do anything about it.

For the state eighth grade examinations over there by the Columbia River, they sent me sealed questions. I had to have one of the parents confirm that the seal wasn't broken before the examination was given. The first year I just had seventh grade, and no eighth grade. The second year I had two students take the eighth grade examination—one passed and one failed. The one that passed had taken it the year before and she was having her review. When I taught at Fairview, students went to the superintendent's office to take the eighth grade examination.

Elsie Hodgson Schnebly.
Frank Schnebly Jr.

A rural teacher was respected and popular in her community, and I think that was something of special value. At social gatherings, the teacher kind of took the lead. On Friday evenings, for example, we held literary meetings, with programs, spoken pieces, and singing. Teachers visited the parents—all the parents—and this was a special part of a family's social life. They all asked the teacher over for Sunday dinner. By doing these things a teacher got to know the children and community better. If a teacher had any problems with students, the parents always seemed to take her word for it. They knew you meant the best for their children. I never had difficulties in that regard; they were always nice.

To some those were the good old days, when "the world was young!" When we still had little country schools scattered over the hills and valleys. The days when elderly people, if they couldn't support themselves, moved in with their children, or, dread the thought, went "over the hills to the poorhouse." The days when a woman's ankles should be unseen. When it was no disgrace to be poor, but it was dishonorable to take charity. It was a more simple life, but with wonderful simple pleasures. Those were the days when families worked together and sang together.

2

Woodpecker College

Marie Pierson Lowe, 1914–18

I guess I decided to teach because it was just the thing to do. The Normal School in 1913 was the cheapest college training that one could get. I went two quarters and received a certificate to teach for one year. We didn't have so very much training. But I think we did just as good a job back then, as compared to later when teachers had more instruction.

There wasn't any special preparation for rural school teaching at the time I attended Ellensburg Normal. We did practice teaching, of course. In many of the classes, material was given out that would say, "Now in a school where you have all the grades or a certain number of grades, it would be well to do…." and so on. But that was all. At that time on campus, there was just one other educational building, the Training School, besides the old main building.

I remember Mr. Morgan, the mathematics instructor. He had a notebook in which he'd written out just exactly how to instruct in arithmetic—how to teach addition, how to teach fractions, and so on. He read this to us as we copied it down; then explained further as he went along. I have that old notebook yet. My, that would be frowned upon now—to think of anybody having it down all so automatic. But it worked just as well.

Dr. Munson taught in science. He was really quite wonderful—an old school man. In one of his classes, we had to look at angleworms. We were just beginning and kind of giddy about handling the worms. "Oh," he'd say, "I'd like to have one of those in my buttonhole. I wouldn't mind that at all!" He thought this was pretty funny, but when he chuckled, you couldn't hear anything—he'd only shake.

John P. Munson, professor of biology at the Washington State Normal School, 1914.
Ellensburg Public Library

We knew we'd have to teach in a rural school first. The school that I became interested in, or rather, they were interested in me, was up in Manastash Canyon. The clerk of the board was looking for a teacher, and they were anxious to have someone who could also instruct in music. I'd taken music in school and a little bit of piano. So, I said I could do that. I got the job and more money than any of the other girls. I was lucky. I received $70 a month, and paid all of $18 a month for board. The others got but $65.

My beau, Mr. Lowe, took me on my first trip to the school in a horse and buggy. The school had one room. The instructional equipment included only a blackboard, perhaps 15 feet long and painted black, which was alright, and there was a dictionary, but no other books at all that I remember. The children provided their own books. A water pail with a dipper stood on a little shelf in back where the students also set their lunches and other belongings. Of course, there were the desks and a big stove in the middle of the room, but that was it other than a hand bell. There was no water pump; we dipped water from a creek not too far back from the schoolhouse.

I had six pupils—one in the third grade, two in the seventh, and three in the eighth. Their wide differences in age caused kind of a problem so far as teaching music was concerned. The poor little third grader was as smart as he could be, but he just sat and listened most of the time. There wasn't anything else to do because I couldn't give him very much time.

The Manastash School in 1914.
Ellensburg Daily Record

We really didn't put on many school programs. With such a small number of students, it was too difficult, though parties were held in homes around the locality on special evenings. I used to read to them. I'd acquire different books and on Friday afternoon I'd read or do some other special thing for them. But a big program of any sort was impossible; I'd just try to do little things.

In those years, county wide spelling matches were held in Ellensburg. My, oh my—how I'd drill those kids and try to prepare them to do a good job of spelling. In those times, students also had to take state examinations in different subjects, which was another thing I worked real hard on.

County superintendents tried to get around and inspect all the schools, but, if I remember rightly, they missed me. People just didn't go for a ride up the Manastash during the wetter, colder months when the roads were in poor condition. I always built a fire when the weather was cold, and the local people made sure there was a sufficient woodpile. These people were just as nice as they could be and very good to me.

I boarded at a school board member's home and it was kind of peculiar in some ways. It was a nice little house, and the only one with running water in the area. Water from a spring up on a hill in back was piped in, which was really wonderful. This couple had married the spring before, and the wife turned 16 after I arrived. She really hadn't learned much about cooking before that time. I gained a lot of weight then that I never got rid of because the food was mostly starch, and I was hungry. But we had a good time, and they were fine. I had it a lot better than some people did.

I think there were no more than a half dozen families living in the Manastash when I taught up there. I was a pretty homesick girl, I'll tell you. The nearest telephone was four miles away, the nearest mailbox also four miles away, and I'd never been away from home before. The local people had lived away from most everyone for so long that they'd developed little "picky" things against others. For instance, the owner of one field wouldn't let anyone go through; we all had to go way around.

Along in the winter when bad weather closed in, four or five little parties were held around the neighborhood. Everybody went to the parties and had a good time in just being there. There was such a variation in ages that there wasn't much that they all could do together, but they enjoyed themselves, and the good food, too.

The people up there had few books, and no library of any sort. I knew Mrs. Davidson at the Ellensburg library; she was the city's first librarian. When the library sorted out books they didn't need, she let me take a good many of them. The people in the canyon that winter were so grateful, because they just hadn't had access to books. That was a help to them.

A lot of the folks hunted quite a bit—grouse in the fall, for instance. In the spring, they brought me rattlesnake rattles. They'd go to rock outcrops high up the Manastash and find snakes warming in the sun. There was quite a slaughter, I guess. This was something I didn't exactly much like, but it was nice of them to bring the rattles to me anyway.

The next year, I taught at the Lyons School #14, east of Ellensburg, which was a larger school. It was a one room schoolhouse, but I had students in all of the grades, about 14 children, I think. This was harder for me than teaching just six students divided up in three grades. In that district, all the children went to school. When one family later moved out, however, I lost three grades of students. In these circumstances, it was difficult to give the littlest ones

Lyons School students.
Ellensburg Public Library

much attention, but somehow they absorbed their schooling. You did the best you could.

In this schoolhouse, woodpeckers had gotten inside and pecked holes up in the ceiling; I suppose to nest or maybe find insects. Anyway, they'd pecked holes up high. Eventually, bees entered the holes and built hives. In the winter, as I remember so well, I had to fire up the big stove real hot, since the ceiling was so high. As the heat went up and thawed out the hives, bees flew down into the room. This occurred a number of times during the coldest weather. You can imagine how difficult it was to keep my squirmy students in their seats with bees flying around. But the children finally figured out they wouldn't get stung if they kept still. They called the school "Woodpecker College."

These students also participated in the countywide spelling contest. For quite some time before the spelling match, this was one of the things I really focused on. The students studied real hard; the spelling matches were a good thing.

We held programs, mostly on holidays such as Halloween, Thanksgiving, or Christmas. It was difficult to do very much in these little schools. However, we did have a nice, big Christmas tree with candles on it. Of course, there was no electricity. In those days you didn't give a thought about candles setting a tree on fire. Nothing caught fire and everything went off well. Looking back now and thinking about it, I wonder what would've happened if we'd had a blaze. People brought gifts for the children and there was candy. They had such a wonderful time at the community Christmas party. During the programs, recitations were given and sometimes a little play of some sort.

Basket socials also were held at the schoolhouse, usually with an accompanying student program. The ladies prepared box lunches (each for two people), making them as attractive as possible to get a good price during the auction. Basket socials usually raised money for some needed thing at the school. After the children spoke their pieces, the baskets were auctioned off. If a basket was particularly attractive, and if a certain someone whispered to another special somebody that this was her basket, it might bring a very good price. Many of the beaus knew what kind of box a special gal was bringing. They'd bid it up; then spend a pleasant hour sharing.

All children across the state needed to pass the eighth grade examinations if they wished to enter high school. This was something that students looked forward to, but also dreaded. It was an incentive to study hard for awhile in reading, arithmetic, history, spelling, and physiology.

When I taught at "Woodpecker College" in the winter of 1915–16, the students didn't dare go out into the deep snow unless it was necessary. Some of the children lived a long distance away and it was difficult for the little folks to travel between their homes and the schoolhouse. At times, parents brought

Lyons School, District #14, ca. 1915.
Ellensburg Public Library

On the way to the Lyons School.
Ellensburg Public Library

them in the morning and came for them after school. In a few days, paths would be trodden in the snow and it became less difficult for the children. I remember one time, however, when no students came and I was the only one in the school that day. I lived close by and could get there more easily.

In 1917–18, I was employed to assist Normal School students in the Rural Training Program. I was assigned to a Yakima rural area, in which students from the college were sent to spend a quarter term in the community. A woman living alone in a big house provided the students with room and board. They began with education instruction, and then toward the end of the quarter term they had an opportunity to teach in the local school. At the time, it remained likely they'd have to teach in rural schools for a year or so before getting hired by city schools, which was what most hoped to do.

One time, a local Japanese family was invited to a Halloween party; they brought all sorts of little candies and gifts. This meant so much to all the children in the community because they just didn't have much of these things. The little Japanese children were so happy to think they could be part of it all.

I've always felt there were advantages in having children go to a school in the community where they live, but up to a point. It seems to me that this ties the community together so much more than busing children somewhere else. On the other hand, the children at a large school have a chance to do a lot more things. There are more facilities and equipment than a one-room school could ever have. There are advantages both ways.

3

So Much Fun

FLORENCE FOLTZ FISCHER, 1916–18

A city girl from Tacoma, Washington, who came across the mountains to attend Washington State Normal School in Ellensburg and fell in love with the country and Ray Fischer.

From the first, I enjoyed living in the Kittitas Valley. I thought the wildflowers and everything about this country was wonderful. I liked skating, sleighing, and cutter riding; all those different things. We used to go up to Thorp along the Yakima River and skate. That was where Andy Shultz cut ice and stored it for ice cream. We'd skate, build a bonfire, bake potatoes, and have all kinds of just natural good fun.

We went skiing a great deal. We used wide rubber bands to attach our galoshes or other footwear to the skis and, with a stick for a ski pole, we'd set out. We skied at Manastash, Robinson, and Swauk canyons and had such good times. Robinson Canyon was a special place and I particularly remember the little contests held up there. We had such good times, while practically spending no money at all.

In Tacoma, I had a next door neighbor who'd been over to Ellensburg; this prompted me to attend the Normal School. I'd get an education and a position as a teacher. Just one dormitory (Kamola Hall) and the main building (now Barge Hall) stood on campus in those days. There were about 250 students and out of those around 15 boys. The classes were small with excellent professors who took a personal interest in us. They were concerned about every pupil in every class. I gained a great deal from my studies there. After attending one year and a summer session, and with some earlier credits from the University of Washington, I graduated.

I well remember Miss Grupe, Professor Munson, and Professor Stephens. The latter was just wonderful; I've always said it was just as much fun to attend his classes as going to a movie, because he was so humorous. We had Methods classes and I took quite a bit of art, of which I was fond. This worked out nicely for me later when I taught school. We practiced teaching at the Training School; a supervisor happened in every so often to see what we were doing and if we were doing it right.

There were music requirements, and though I'm really not musical myself, I enjoyed it. Later, when teaching music in school, I had two girls, Dorothy and Helen Hoffman, with wonderful voices. They'd always start off a song and I could join in just fine. So, I didn't have any problem in teaching singing, but I couldn't have done it without them. But I was more interested in art than music.

Getting my first job was easy. My beau, Ray Fischer, took me out and introduced me to the directors at the Cove School and that was it. I didn't have any difficulty, except the teacher who'd been there before had taught Manual Training. I'd have to teach that too, though I hadn't had any instruction in that area.

When I graduated after summer school, I was free for five weeks before the job started. After returning home to Tacoma, I called the Superintendent of Manual Training. "I have to have some practical projects," I told him, "because I'm going to be teaching in the country."

He said, "I can't refer you to anybody, but I'll teach you myself." He lived out at Spanaway Lake, and day after day I went out there by streetcar.

Florence Foltz, 1916.
Richard Fischer

Cove School, ca. 1916.
Ellensburg Public Library

When I started at the Cove School, these big, tall, eighth-grade boys looked at me and said, "Can you teach Manual Training?"

I replied, "I surely can or I wouldn't be here."

We built little animal feeders and various other small projects for farm and home, which the students could quickly complete. The school had good equipment. I got by, and the directors asked me to come back.

The Cove School stood on the corner of Cove and Richards roads—a two room building with a bell, and a delightful place. A most interesting lady, Ethel Anderson, taught the primary work. We enjoyed working together. She was talented and taught music, while I focused on art instruction and Manual Training.

Christmas celebrations were special. The school had a stage where the children presented their programs, while my Mr. Fischer dressed up as Santa Claus. By then I knew most everyone in the community.

One time, the ladies held an old fashioned box social to raise money for the school. They prepared fancy box lunches that were auctioned off. Whoever bought a lady's box was her companion for lunch.

It was the duty of a teacher to prepare the older pupils for passing the eighth grade examinations or they couldn't go on to high school. If a teacher didn't accomplish this, it was held against her. I worked hard on this all the time and didn't have any trouble with my pupils passing.

Next, I taught at the Woldale School. It also was a two-room school, and quite a large building. Elizabeth Richards was the primary teacher, while I served as the upper grades instructor. I taught the fifth, sixth, seventh, and eighth grades, just like at the Cove School. Maintaining discipline was easy; I could always talk things over with students. One time at the Cove School, two fifth-grade boys threw spitballs on the ceiling. I invited them to stay after school and had them climb a ladder to remove the spitballs. I never had trouble of that kind again.

The schoolhouses were heated by big, old-fashioned stoves burning wood or coal. The older boys tended the fire. They were very good about bringing in fuel and keeping the stove going. Many of the children arrived by a horse and buggy, or rode horseback to school in those days. Some tied their horses in back of the building where they stood for the day.

The Woldale School had hot lunches, prepared by the upper grade girls and served right there in the large building. This was a big success, as a good hot lunch was greatly appreciated. I can't remember for sure, but I wouldn't be surprised if the district furnished the meals. The district stood between two railroads and was rather prosperous. There were funds for anything we needed. When we wanted electric Christmas lights for our tree, why we had them—anything we'd ask for!

The school served as the social center of the community and parties were held there every so often. People played whist and, after sandwiches and coffee, we would dance. In 1917 after America entered World War I, a number of local people thought we shouldn't spend time dancing, but rather knit

Florence (left, front row) on outing to the Vantage petroglyphs on the Columbia River, 1916.
Richard Fischer

clothes for servicemen and sell war bonds, and that's what I did in my extra time. The parties stopped, but I think resumed again after the war.

I received $60 each month—a quite normal salary—when teaching at the Cove School. My family was in California then, and I was able to purchase passage by boat and visit them, plus cover my room and board, new clothes, and everything else with that $60 a month salary. When moving over to the Woldale School, the pay increased by $10 to $70, then $80, and so on—a perfectly good salary at the time.

The families were all farmers around the districts where I taught. When coming back from Tacoma to take my first job, I boarded on the Charlie Richards farm. At that time farming was diversified; I was amazed because they had sheep, cattle, gardens, everything. Farmers could practically get by without buying anything in town.

Sometimes I'd visit around at the homes if parents had suggestions or questions about their children. I remember one parent who wanted her eighth grade daughter to take some ninth grade work. The mother felt that her daughter was capable of going on; the girl was bright. I said I'd be glad to give her this extra work. So, I did.

I believe that those children who were more interested in education are the ones that get ahead in life. I remember one youngster who was a good pupil, but a daydreamer. I'd have to nudge him every so often and kind of bring him to. Then he'd go on. Another student was good at fixing things. When anything needed to be done at the school, I'd call on him. I made use of him because he was very clever. I think it is the people who really want to get ahead that eventually do.

Florence Foltz Fischer.
Richard Fischer

People in these communities were close-knit and very respectful to teachers. On Saturdays, they'd drive me to town, as I didn't have a car. Now that was something special— going to town! I'd sit up in front with the driver. I had many good times in Ellensburg. I was going with Mr. Fischer then, so I had lots of fun. At Woldale, they also gave me an engagement shower.

We'd also take trips to the mountains—into the Mount Stuart country or to Snoqualmie Pass. Driving up to Snoqualmie Pass was a thrill because of the narrow road with a lake below; I always was glad when we got back home. Blewett Pass in those days was even worse because of its very poor road. I also went horseback riding; trips to Umptaneum Falls were special. We'd cook breakfast out in the open and do things like that. It was a very rustic life. You really just wore camp clothes. We went to lots of parties and dances, as well as many, many picnics. I enjoyed everything we did.

In the years since I taught at the Woldale School, one former student has kept in touch for over a half-century, sending cards for Christmas, my birthday, and on other occasions. She was gifted in writing themes and had a wonderful imagination. She wrote such interesting stories. She has kept in contact with me all these years.

4

You Get That There Certificate

GRACE HANKS McQUEEN, 1918–22

I'm left handed and was punished in school for this. In the second grade, I was slapped because I used my left hand. I tried to write in a right handed slant even though I wanted to use the left handed slant. Occasionally, I wrote three ways in one word—straight up and down, left, and right.

When I finished Normal School, Professor Smyser said, "Now Grace, you're a good student and you'll make a good teacher, but what is the matter with your writing?"

I told him what was the matter.

"Well," he says, 'Why don't you write like yourself?"

See, that was very advanced. Today we tell a child to write as he or she wishes and be themselves, but in those days we tried hard to fit into accepted patterns. The accepted pattern was to write with a right handed slant.

Mr. Smyser's advice, "Write like yourself," was wonderful.

During my first year at the Normal School, the instructors still operated under the old regime, if I may call it that. Professor Wilson and others were theoretical people. They were gentle, sweet people, but they were almost living in the clouds. They didn't really want to be business-like, or do anything other than just their one object—to give us what we needed to go out and teach little children. I thought it wasn't very progressive.

Things started changing in my second year at the college when Professor Stephens arrived. He was quite a different person. Several others came, too, that sort of broke up the old ways of teaching. Stephens wanted the college to adopt different courses. To me, education classes were always dry, but I remember one thing from his class in education. He said, "Now all the things I've told you don't make much difference, but remember, when you feel your worst, to put on your best!"

Professor Stephens.
The Kooltuo (1917)

This sounded rather strange to us as students, but it has since been one of my principles throughout life. When I feel down, I try to dress up or get my hair done a little better, or at least shine my shoes. It helps.

When President Black arrived at the college, he was quite advanced in his planning and wanted the institution to progress. He tried putting the college on more of a business basis, which he eventually did. Black kept pushing for better facilities and buildings, and hiring instructors from outside the area who would bring new outlooks.

During this period, there suddenly was talk about whether or not the state government would close the Normal School. At the time, there were three state normal schools—Ellensburg, Cheney, and Bellingham [today's Central Washington, Eastern Washington, and Western Washington universities]. A proposal called for changing Ellensburg's college into a girls' reform school. My father was serving in the legislature at the time and worked hard to get a library building for the campus, which he said would assure Ellensburg's retention of the college. It worked, and was the start for the authorization of more buildings.

In my second year, 17 men and around 300 women attended the Normal School. I knew every one of them. Many students lived off campus, renting for room and board. The college needed more residence space for students, since there was but one dormitory, Kamola Hall, for the girls and a made-over house called Eswin Hall for the boys. Dormitory living allowed the college to exert more control over the students' lives, which I thought was a good thing because the student body was pretty young.

Every class at the Normal School was slanted toward preparing students to be teachers, particularly in elementary education. The teaching curriculum was for only one- and two-year programs. At the end of my first year, I decided to take a job at Crab Creek, way out from nowhere in the Columbia Basin. I told them I'd take that school.

When I went home, however, my father said, "I won't let you go out there. You're not even 18 and I won't let you go out there in that God forsaken country. You just go on back to school."

We had an old neighbor in town who talked loudly, and sometimes I'd ride to school with him. He'd say, "Whatever else you do, you get that there certificate!"

Well, I could've gone out and taught with a one year elementary certificate, but I went ahead and finished the two year course. My father and I then drove out to the Lower Naneum School for an interview with the directors. They later called and told me I had the job.

Lower Naneum School, District #20.
Ellensburg Public Library

Lower Naneum was a nice little school—a typical one room building with cloakrooms on each side, one for the boys and one for girls. When the children arrived in the morning, they'd sit in front of the large stove and put their feet up to the heat, until the room was warm. A sort of storeroom at the back had a little hot plate to warm something up or make coffee for school or community events. Three structures stood out back—the boys' toilet, girls' toilet, and a little horse barn with attached shed for storing wood and coal. The teacher was supposed to maintain the premises and generally be responsible. Though some meetings occurred in the schoolhouse, the big community gatherings were held over at Fairview Hall.

There was a wonderful, dependable eighth grader, Carl Gustafson, who mostly attended to the stove. I had 11 boys and 4 girls, with students in all of the grades. The demand on my time to teach all eight levels prevented some of the good natured competition between the grades. However, every once in a while I'd double-up on classes and we'd have fun with a spelling match, or a history facts contest, and things like that. All the children were cooperative.

The pupils brought their own books, usually purchased second-hand or passed down from an older brother, sister, or relative. If families had to buy new books, they went to the Craig Wheeler Bookstore in town, which stocked all the required texts for the county schools.

In the wintertime, I loved to skate and slide in the snow, and the children did too. The Crockett pond was located about a mile from the school. When conditions were just right for skating, I'd say to the children at noon, "Let's take our lunches with us today. We'll skip 15 minutes of our afternoon reading and all go down to the pond and skate."

We hiked down, all eating our lunches on the way. Of course, I really wasn't very much older than the bigger students. We'd take a sled or two and pull along the youngest children who were too little to walk that far. We pulled kids on the sleds around the frozen pond and, of course, we'd skate. Then we'd rush to get back by 1:15. They'd dive into their work and get it done.

In the autumn of 1918, the world war yet raged in Europe. The first big community event I participated in was a War Bond program. This was a patri-

---

Excerpt from Grace Hanks Diary, September 1918[1]

[*On Tuesday*] I promised to have a program ready for [*Friday night*]…and went to work. The song "Heroes" was one and then we worked out in pantomime, "The Caging of the Kaiser." Carl was the Kaiser and did fine with his paper helmet & real sword while the Kaiser took all the French children's toys, wrecked the Belgians' houses, etc. The Russian bear tagged around with a happy smile about 6 ft from the Kaiser. Margaret, Willie & Walter were Belgians & Wanetta, Loila & Ruby the French. The Kaiser fought with John Bull in his stovepipe hat & bright red coat, light trousers, etc. The English (Roland) could not beat the Kaiser but saved his boat (which indicated British Navy). The K. was so puffed over his last victory that he tackled a bunch of American soldiers (Lawrence, Donald, Earnest & Roy) who immed. went after him with their guns and put him in a big cage & carried him off.

Grace Hanks McQueen, 1924.
Barbara McQueen

otic effort to encourage citizens to purchase national bonds, which helped fund America's involvement. When people from the community gathered, I was nervous because I felt particularly responsible for the bond drive. The whole neighborhood came. Mrs. Mahan, the wife of a prominent doctor in town, arrived with the musicians. When we stood up and sang together, I didn't make any sound. I just opened and closed my mouth because I was so awed by Mrs. Mahan's beautiful voice. We sold bonds, and then it wasn't long until the Armistice was declared on November 11, 1918. The war's ending was a real wonderful thing to happen.

Everything then continued fine, until along in January when the worldwide flu epidemic struck our community. Two or three people died right away. The school was closed for six weeks. On weekends, I'd been driving back and forth to Ellensburg with family and friends (including the D.D. Schneblys, where I boarded), so now I stayed home for awhile.

The flu was horrible, and no community escaped it. When I went downtown, I wore a mask over my mouth and nose as advised. I didn't contract the flu that year, but in the next year I got very sick.

I anxiously wanted to make up for lost time when school opened again. I went to Mr. Gustafson, the head of the school board, saying, "May I teach on Washington's Birthday and Saturdays to make up time?"

He replied, "Why don't you forget it?"

District #6, 1919.
Barbara McQueen

So I did. The two eighth graders graduated regardless. They had to take the state examinations, which were tough. They needed my drilling. There were some good things about those tests, but also bad things, especially regarding an emphasis on small facts. For me, it was a matter of teaching the eighth graders to memorize particular things, which at their age wasn't something they were particularly interested in doing. Anyway, the school year was successfully completed.

I would've returned to the Lower Naneum School for the 1919–20 term, but I wanted to be nearer home as my folks were going to be away. So I took the School #6 near Ellensburg, with 26 children in all eight grades. I remember injuring my elbow and I

The Spanish Flu

[*November 15, 1918*] Carpenters and Sheppard are sick with the "flu"—one on each side of school house... [*November 18*] Went to school in the best of spirits. Had the honorable number of five pupils. The rest (excepting Carpenters) were afraid of the flu. In the evening I learned that Mr. Bartlett [*the superintendent*] had discontinued the school for wk...[*December 4*] Last night mama called me...She said that there were 70 cases of the flu in the H.S. and 3 teachers and there are 30 cases of small pox and several cases of scarlet fever... [*January 12, 1919*] Amy Scone, a girl I had gone to Normal with and had taught at No. 1... died from pneumonia following influenza. I can't believe it... [*January 1919*] Got word today that Irene Hartman Cooke had died from pneumonia. She left a little baby and her husband as well as her parents. I thot a lot of Irene. She was a sweet fine girl and a lovely musician. Also Ada Hendricks, another schoolmate of mine who was teaching at Thorp, came home and died from the "flu." That is three schoolmates in a week and there are many others dying... [*February 18*] Eton Galloner died from the flu while on her wedding trip. She had been married ten days. Her mother died 2 mo. ago from flu & Eton was the oldest in the family. She was in my class at high school and in Normal. We were very good friends. She was well and happy. That makes 4 class-mates in a very short time.—*Grace Hanks diary.*

"My little car I drive to school."
Barbara McQueen

Recess at the District #6 school.
Barbara McQueen

could hardly write. I had my little car by that time, which I'd park overnight at home in a little open garage that formerly was a horse barn. It was difficult getting my car started on some of the fiercely cold days.

I next took a job out at Kittitas where I worked for two years. I taught just three grades in the classroom; I really enjoyed getting away from teaching all eight grades at one time. The Kittitas community was just one big wonderful family—there were no arguments, school wise or otherwise. There was a group of young people there, mostly single, and we had lots of parties and even put on a play, "The Arrival of Kitty," followed by a box supper. Everyone came; the crowd was enormous. We made $236.50, which I'll never forget, and gave it to the town for a children's project, every penny of it. We were so proud of ourselves! In winter, we went tobogganing out on the Clerf Hills, where the men cleared a space and you had to go over two bumps. It was lots of fun, but a little risky sometimes.

"The way I dressed for the lead part in 'The Arrival of Kitty' when I taught at Kittitas. The little pup is real. He belongs to Dad."
Barbara McQueen

In those years, most of the larger towns such as Ellensburg only hired teachers with experience. Young teachers, of course, could only begin their careers by starting out in rural schools. Country schoolteachers had to be good, instructing every child from five years old and up. In town, youngsters didn't enter school until they were six, but in the country they could start at five. Many rural teachers also taught first year high school courses to the oldest students. Some of the older boys could be big fellows and rambunctious; they often had to help out with farming and hadn't been able to attend much school. Rural teachers needed to control them. If not, a school board might simply let a teacher go, even in mid-year. A rural school teacher in those days had to be effective and capable.

When I taught at my first school, I remember thinking very proudly about how well they paid me at $90 a month. I was as pleased as I could be. Of course, living expenses weren't so much back then.

Mr. Bartlett, the county superintendent, held a quite powerful position. I remember one of his inspections at the District #6 school. I had a boy who'd normally behave himself beautifully, but when someone visited he wanted to show off. On this occasion, the superintendent came in and sat for half a day. Evidently this boy started doing pranks, or "monkeyshine" as we called it then. I didn't give any attention to him because I knew the boy pretty well and his antics were harmless.

But at recess the superintendent said, "Would you like me to take that boy out behind the woodshed and give him a little paddling?"

I said, "Oh, he doesn't bother me. Don't worry about him because I can handle him. I just don't pay any attention because it's the way to make him get tired of it quicker."

"Well," he says, "You're probably right." So he didn't spank him.

Mrs. Lee, another superintendent, visited me at Kittitas. When she walked in, I was teaching a class in Physiology about the hazards of tobacco use. Personally, I didn't like tobacco; it almost always made me ill. I was telling the third grade children that it would just ruin their hearts if they used too much tobacco, especially smoking.

Kittitas High School, 1927.
Ellensburg Public Library

When I finished, Mrs. Lee said, "Why Grace that was the best lesson I've ever heard on the use of tobacco."

Well, I was kind of pleased, but also I must've been sort of over-enthusiastic about the issue.

The holiday programs were a wonderful thing for children in rural schools. There always was a Christmas program and treats. I gave every child an opportunity to participate or perform in some way. It could be difficult for some of them to stand up and be the focus of an audience, especially their first time. Children would get up and they'd work through their roles; some were terribly embarrassed, but they thought it through and came to like doing something extra and different. They learned to enjoy performing for parents and friends. They also received a broadening of interests, such as: What do they do in Sweden for Christmas? I remember the stories of the birds on Christmas morning, which was something many children never heard before.

I recall the spring program I arranged during my first year of teaching. Even though we were short of time, due to the six week flu closure, we decided to hold a program. We worked and practiced on dialogues and plays, and we had costumes. I went to old Auntie Larsen's place with some of the children to pick out costumes. The elderly lady had passed away, but the clothes she'd brought from the old country were still in her home. We picked out capes and other clothing for the children to wear in the program.

We wanted to practice in Fairview Hall where the program would be held. The hall stood about two miles from the Lower Naneum School. The four girls and I rode in the little Schnebly girls' old buggy. The boys, all 10 of them, had to walk. It was a warm day early in May. One little boy said, "I'm not going to walk that far." The oldest boy took him off to one side; I don't know what was said, but they all walked. We rehearsed down there twice. The program was about 1½ hours long, and every child had plenty of parts.

When we put on the program, Fairview Hall was completely filled with parents and friends. They were so appreciative of our program. Then the local women did their part, serving cake, ice cream, and coffee, all a wonderful treat. Someone then sat down at the piano and I believe they even danced a little before finally going home. I was so pleased to see every person in the community in attendance.

Along with the joys of teaching, there were some sad stories, too. Attitudes toward teachers were good in the districts where I taught, but in one community there were two people, like you sometimes hear about, going around looking for things to criticize. But I heard so little of this; it was almost

End of Year Program, Lower Naneum School

June 1 School is out. Everything finaled up, etc. I am at home—riding horseback—sewing and taking life easy. We had a big programme Wed. May 21, 1919. I got more compliments for that program than I expect to for any one thing I do again. There were at least 135 people there (from 4 districts). The children did splendidly. The program was as follows:

Lovely May (song)—whole school
Danish Dance of Greeting—whole school
Little Johnny Jump Up by Margarite Stampfly dressed as a yellow violet...
Elvin Walty (duet)—Wanetta and Loila
The Kitty—Carl Cooke
Granpa's Watch—Willie C.
Jolly Whistler—whole school
The Arbutus (with motions)—whole school
Brave Warrior—Ruby Gustafson
Patience Works Wonders—Nellie S.
Fickle Little Butterfly—solo by Lawrence Carpenter
"Goin' Somewheres"—dialogue on train—Ruby & Donald dressed as an old
     queer couple from country—absolutely humorous costumes
Long Boy—Willie Carpenter—great hit—little six year old good voice—can't
     talk plain—sang it twice
Audubon Sassiety—Walter
Santa Lucia—whole school
Shoemakers' Dance—10 children (very pretty)
Little Ruby's Piano—Ruby & Roland
How to Do It—Roy Eggert—cute roast on dramatized speaking
Irish Lilt (jig)—Roland Gustafson & Fred Stampfly
Boat Song—whole school
Indian playlet –last thing

The Indian playlet was beautiful. We had a fire—red tissue paper—lanterns & sticks—ten Indian braves with feathers around their heads seated in circle around fire—Loila dressed as a beautiful Indian Maiden stood at back & recited "Childhood of Hiawatha" then sat down & rocked the little Carpenter baby Indian fashion while Wanetta sang Ojibway Indian lullaby. Then girls left the stage and boys sang "Playing Indian" & gave a big yell at the end.

We had a bean race between representatives from each of the 4 schools. Fairview beat—.

Autograph cards and pencils proved to be jolly & a fine mixer. Mrs. D.D. Schnebly got the 1st prize (box of candy) & Dorsey Bregg the Booby prize which was a stick of candy in a big box. The ladies served sandwitches, cake and coffee in great abundance.—*Grace Hanks diary.*

impossible for me to believe it. In my years of teaching, the community took me in like just one of the family.

One time in mid year, I had a new little boy assigned to my class. His father had taken a job with a local farmer. This boy wanted to learn. Oh, he wanted to learn so badly! He had a good mind, but had been kept out of school, and he was very sad. Some of us helped with the physical things that we could do for the family. When the family finally left—they practically departed overnight—he was taken out of school. I wanted to help him so much; he was so sad. He had a stripe mark across his face, and I'd swear he'd probably been whip-lashed.

Two other children in my room that year also had serious problems—a little girl dying of cancer, and a nervous little boy. Talk about being emotionally upset, he was in terrible shape. His mother had been killed in an automobile accident some time before. By hook and crook and everything else, I finally found out he'd overheard his father say he thought he might have cancer of the stomach. So, this little boy thought his father was dying of cancer. He wasn't, and had indigestion or something, but he didn't have cancer.

The little girl who had cancer eventually did pass away. She was one of the bravest children I've ever known.

Now to return to the first child that I spoke of—the little boy that was so sad. One night I took him into the office and said, "You feel pretty sorry for yourself don't you?"

I indeed felt sorry for him, too, but said again, "You feel pretty sorry for yourself don't you?"

He didn't answer but just kind of hung his head.

I then said, "I want to tell you about two other children in our own room...what they're going through." So I told him about the girl with cancer and the nervous little boy whose mother had been killed.

I said, "You don't have anything like that. You have some troubles, but you're going to have to grow up and be a man, and you're probably going to have to help your family. They're going to need your help." That seemed to perk him up, and he was such a changed boy after that.

One day this boy was invited to a birthday party at the Sabins, who lived right across the street from the school. It would be after school, and just about all the boys in my room were invited. The Sabins handed out invitations, and gave one to this boy, too. He lived a considerable distance away. On the morning of the appointed day, he told me he couldn't go to the party; he had to go home.

I said, "Why?"

Wintertime at District #6, 1919.
Barbara McQueen

He replied, "Well, my folks said I had to come home. I can't go to the party."

"If I'd call them could you go?"

"No, don't call them, I can't go."

I sent word over to Mrs. Sabin that he couldn't come. But she called up the parents, saying, "If I bring him home can he go?"

They said yes.

After the party she piled that bunch of boys into a car and drove out there where he lived. He got to go to the party. I think he'd never been to one before.

It was a joy to help little folks learn and prepare for life. There are a lot of reasons why some children excel and others don't. Of course, a little child should be well fed and not mentally damaged at home before coming to school. To be good learners, they can't be absorbed by worries. A child can't live in a house where there is strife, sorrow, and division, and be expected to come to school with a free and open mind, ready to learn. Children need a certain calmness about them and assurance of appreciation.

The children who were responsible in school were shaped by positive community and family values. They wanted to do their work, play fair, and learn. The ones who were encouraged to take on these responsibilities in their family life were happy, plus they had a shoulder to lean on at home.

I also believe, in all honesty, that they needed a prop to blame if they're uncertain or think they can't do some things. I heard many a little boy and girl say, "I can't do that because my mother won't let me," or, "My dad says I shouldn't do that."

They said this instead of, "I don't want to do that," or "I don't think it's the thing to do."

Occasionally, when their own shortcomings came up in some regard, they needed assurance of someone who they could blame. This is alright for developing young minds—that's what parents and teachers are for. Children gradually develop their own strength by observing responsible adults. The old line of Danish families that had settled in the countryside where I taught were proud of their youngsters, who developed a sense of fair play, hard work, and honesty.

Note

1. Grace Hanks McQueen's Lower Naneum diary provided courtesy of her daughter, Barbara McQueen, of Bethesda, Maryland.

5

They Needed a Teacher Right Then

FERNE CHARLTON HABERMAN, 1919–22

I was working with my uncle in a shoe store, but the pay wasn't very good and I had to do something else. I wanted to attend business school but didn't have the money to pay for it. So instead, I enrolled at the Normal School, which was free to the public, though students had to meet admission standards. There were only several boys when I started there. The rest of them were girls.

I attended the summer session and continued on in the next quarters, and by springtime had a teaching job up in the Okanogan country. They called me into the office and asked if I'd take the Okanogan job. They needed a teacher right then! I agreed and over the weekend I packed up and started out. There were a few Ellensburg teachers in the Okanogan locality, which made it rather nice for me.

The school stood about six miles from Tonasket; the superintendent took me there the first day. A local housewife had been filling in temporarily as the teacher. The superintendent wanted me to take over that very day. This frightened me, since I hadn't really received any teaching practice during my time at the Normal School. But the next day, after I got started on my own, it was fine.

It was a typical rural one-room building with about 25 pupils. The school had been closed down quite a bit; they had a hard time getting teachers. The first year I taught until the last of July to make up for lost time due to the earlier closure. I found that books were scarce, but the superintendent was good about resolving this, especially in the last part of the school year. He brought out books from the city school after it closed for the summer. After instructing grade-schoolers during the day, I taught high school courses—Algebra and English—after school to some older students who couldn't travel to a high school. Parents objected when I taught high school courses during regular hours so we held them after class. I received no extra pay for this.

Ferne
Patrick Haberman

When we rang the school's big bell, it could be heard for miles around. I think there were five school bells that could be heard in a wide radius up there—a beautiful sound. All the students wanted to ring the bell. It was rung at 8:30 a.m.—a kind of reminder for any students that were lingering and having fun on the way to school. The students walked; it was a little valley. The bell also rang for the end of each recess and at noon. In those days, students generally were formed into lines before marching into the schoolhouse. I don't know why, maybe it was a little more orderly.

I didn't arrange any programs, but I did take the youngsters on field trips and we held a year-end picnic. I'd take them up into the hills or along the creek. These were wonderful outings, with no particular aim in mind.

The Tonasket community involved the students in something rather unusual for a school. The Indians had a graveyard there and sometimes they'd let us bring the children to attend a burial. It was a good experience for them and right in the neighborhood, too. Some Indian youngsters attended my school. In fact, I went to school with the father of one of my Indian pupils. These children were just like the other students—some were bright and some not so bright.

I started at $80 per month, which was good wages at the time. They wanted me to return and I would've gone back, but then I was offered a job at the Lower Naneum School back in the Kittitas Valley, and with more pay—I think that year I received $100.

After teaching at Lower Naneum, I next taught at the Upper Naneum School #18 and then the Edgemont-Thrall School #6. (The Upper Naneum has since burned, Lower Naneum was made into a home, and I believe Edgemont-Thrall was later moved.) These were one room buildings with cloakrooms, one for the boys and one for girls. I always rang the bell at 8:30; then we started at 9. If a school didn't have a kitchen, they'd add a little room and provide a stove for hot lunches. The schools were pretty much the same pattern.

More library books were available in the Kittitas Valley. Upper Naneum, in particular, had a nice library. When I was a child attending a rural school,

Upper Naneum School, District #18.
Ellensburg Public Library

I remember the box socials, when money was raised for purchasing library books and playground equipment.

The students brought their own textbooks, tablets, and pencils to class. Some families had little money and it was difficult for them to purchase even a tablet or pencil. If a student didn't have these things, the teacher always had some on hand—paid for out of her own pocket.

Programs were required in the valley—about three a year. These always included Christmas and Thanksgiving programs, and a picnic, which generally required singing. That's one of the things I especially liked about teaching—in the morning we'd sing some songs before starting classes. I remember a piano that was given to us. A teacher needed to at least know how to use a pitch pipe, and be able to lead students in music. Most every one of any age in those days sang, or at least tried to sing.

I did my own janitor work, but generally I had assistance. Some of the youngsters would stay and give a hand, which was helpful. The students and I prepared the hot lunches, unless parents brought them in. A lot of the time parents liked to come and cook for us. All I'd have to say to warn a youngster was, "Well, if you don't get that done, you can go peel carrots." This had the desired effect.

All the children in the district were required to attend school. If a student failed to arrive, the clerk went to determine why they hadn't appeared, or if they needed assistance in coming.

Teachers were expected to visit each of the students' homes at least once a year and stay overnight. It was alright—a way to become acquainted with the parents. They helped quite a lot sometimes, but a teacher sometimes had difficulties. Some parents might think their youngster wasn't being treated fairly in the classroom.

Arguments sometimes arose among the students as they went back and forth to school—mostly teasing, and sometimes rough language. When they went home and talked about it, I suspect they blew things up a bit to their parents. Then, a parent would come storming up to the schoolhouse while I still was there. These disputes could be hard to settle. I'd get the parents and youngsters together to straighten things out. Generally this worked, but I remember one little boy saying, "Yes, I did it, so you're just going to have to whip me." Which I hated doing.

Each year, eighth grade students took a state examination to qualify for entering high school. After a teacher taught a year, she generally knew what needed to be stressed when preparing the pupils. After students took the test, a teacher could review the exams. Eventually, I think, the state made allowances if a student didn't pass in all the topics. Sometimes they'd let them enter high school if they failed in one part where the student had difficulty. At the time, rural students were required to take the exam at the county superintendent's office. Later on, they sent the tests out to the rural areas, where one of the directors would sit in and observe. There were better results that way.

Teachers were hired by school directors, who in turn were responsible to the county superintendent. The county superintendent visited once a year. At first I dreaded this, but my cousin was superintendent one year, and after she came and visited, I didn't mind it anymore. A teacher generally had some idea about when the superintendent would come, and could groom the kids in what they were supposed to do and how to act.

When I taught at the town of Cle Elum, a larger school, one of the teachers we all liked was let go. The directors said they fired him and I suppose they must've had reason, but that's something we never found out. In those days, people didn't talk much about these things. We felt badly, because he was so much fun to be around on the playground. On the playground, by the way, I was a good baseball player. I broke two fingers.

Teachers could sort of develop their own social life on their own. They were free to do as they wanted, just so long as it wasn't anything that caused too much talk. Teachers participated in neighborhood get-togethers to sing, and there were lots of these. Later, local people started holding card parties, and, of course, a teacher was expected to go. A teacher was supposed to attend all social events in a community.

I don't think parents paid much attention to the curriculum. They left this up to the state, the county superintendent, and the teachers. There was no parental interference in that regard. But if parents could assist in some way, they were available and very helpful.

Cle Elum was different from the rural schools where I taught in that there were more disciplinary problems. However, I had the principal and the superintendent to help out. I only had one grade, although I could do some switching with another teacher. I enjoyed teaching geography, but I didn't like English, so I traded these subjects with another teacher. This helped the children out, too, providing them with a little better instruction in each subject.

I think education starts in the home. If there's a spark there, why, it goes better for a child. If they've had pretty good home training, most can learn. I only had a few who had a difficult time learning. Some wanted to quit school. I'd try to keep them from dropping out, until the superintendent would say, "It's just no use, don't try anymore because they don't want do anything."

But years later, I'd happen to see them, and they'd say, "Oh, I wished I hadn't dropped out of school." At least they had the right attitude later.

A good aspect of a rural school was the fact that students pitched in and assisted each other. I had upper grade youngsters that just loved to help the younger ones. A lot of the instruction for each of the grades was done on the blackboard; the older grades could review their past lessons when they had been in the lower grades, and the younger pupils could see what they'd be learning in the future. They were so willing to be helpful.

I didn't have time to give each student much individual attention; when I had all eight grades to teach, it was hard sometimes. In the primary grades, pupils needed to do more things with their hands. In the upper grades, it was more study. Sometimes, a little pressure had to be put on the eighth graders who had the state exams ahead of them. But the in-between kids listened to what I taught the upper grades and they helped the little ones. So I really think a child in a rural school didn't lose too much from getting limited attention from a teacher.

6

They'll Throw Her Right through the Window, First Day

HELEN "NELL" DONALD HADLEY, 1920–22

Bright eyed and bushy tailed, diminutive 98-year-old Nell whisked around the room bringing out albums, books, and pictures to add to the interview, eager to share her life experiences. That she was a small positive force to be reckoned with in 1920 was soon discovered by the potentially unruly boys at Roza School.

My name is really Helen but everybody calls me "Nell" or "Nellie." We came from Scotland in 1911 when I was 10 years old. My dad had received a letter from my uncle George saying, "Why don't you come to America? You'll get further ahead than in Scotland where property is just handed down to the oldest son."

We had a little difficulty getting here from Scotland, but my folks were determined to come and we did. The ship got lost coming over when the vessel's compass broke. We went too far north and were among icebergs for awhile. It took us 10 days to cross the ocean. There were many people stopped at Ellis Island, but all my dad had to do was show the letter from Uncle George: "You have a job and a home, so come on over." We went right on through.

Uncle George had married a Tjossem but they had no youngsters. They lived out in the Denmark district of eastern Kittitas County—so we'd come from Scotland to "Denmark," to live among all the Tjossems, Petersens, Jensens, and Sorensons. I'd been wondering if I'd be accepted, but I immediately had friends.

My mother eventually became well known in the valley for doing a lot of nursing. They called her "Auntie Donald." When first coming to this country, she started helping out with the birthing of babies. The doctor would come out and they'd meet at an expectant mother's house and deliver the baby. Then she'd stay in the home for two weeks, which in those days was the expected time for a mother to recover from giving birth.

Our Scottish accent made for my speaking a kind of broken English, at least to the ears of the other kids. It wasn't as easy for the other kids to understand me, as it was for me to understand them. I usually could figure out what they were saying, except one day when they held their hands up and asked the teacher if they could go to the library. I'd never heard that word. I wondered what it was. I could see that they went in and got a book, so I held up my hand. The teacher said, "Yes?" I replied, "Can I luke at a buke?" Of course, the kids all laughed, but I could out run and also out spell most of them.

Community spelling bees were held in those days. My brother was a fifth grader and I was in the third grade. We joined the spelling group and came out tops. I was a third grader who beat the ex-school teachers. After attending Denmark Elementary, I went to Kittitas High School and graduated with honors. Enrolling at the Normal School, I took up elementary education, went there one year, earned a teaching certificate, and taught for two years before going back to college. I attended another year and graduated in 1923.

I first taught at Roza, beginning in 1920. It was a one room school located down in the Yakima River canyon, quite a few miles south of my folks' place

Flag stop station.
Ellensburg Public Library

near Thrall. It stood right on the river and next to the Northern Pacific Railroad. I traveled between Thrall and Roza on the train because no road went down there, except for a roundabout route through Shuskin and into a field.

The president of the school board, Mary Roberts, interviewed me and offered the job at $125 a month. Mrs. Roberts did a lot of things at Roza. In addition to serving as the school board president, she was the postmistress, took the town census, ran a little merchandise store, and had the flag to stop the train for passengers. I boarded at the Roberts' home for $25 a month.

I hadn't been to Roza before and didn't know what to expect, but I didn't run into any difficulties. I might not have been so lucky, because the year before they'd had problems. The teacher was too lenient. Of course, this was my first year and I really didn't know what to expect.

The clerk told me that she'd talked to her husband, who said, "Well, you're not going to hire that little woman are you?"

She told him, "I think I will."

"Oh," he said. "They'll throw her right through the window, first day."

If she hadn't told me this, they might have! She had me on my toes. I laid the law down right from the start of school, so the students didn't get by with much.

If I wanted to go home on a Friday afternoon, I'd go to the post office, ask for the flag, and then I flagged the train down. After riding to Thrall, there generally was a kind elderly man, Mr. Conners, waiting for me. As I think back on it, he probably wasn't that old, but he was a fine gentleman. He'd wait there with his hand car at Thrall, then he'd pump me down the tracks to the first crossing and I only had to walk half way home. I had a lot of fun like this along with my teaching.

Our family farm stood about a mile from Thrall, just above where the Yakima canyon begins. We lived almost at the end of Woodhouse Loop Road, as it later was named. Being close to the railroad, we heard trains going by all the time. We could hear them tooting at three crossings before they reached Thrall. On a Sunday evening, I'd catch a train at Thrall and they'd let me off at Roza.

When applying for the job, I had no idea what the Roza School was going to look like, but I thought it wouldn't be much. It was a one room building, but it was well kept—indeed, very well kept. There was a library behind the entrance. The desks had inkwells and seats that flipped up. They were all screwed down in rows to floor boards. It wasn't difficult to slide or carry them to the side of the room to make space for a dance or other event. Outside stood two outhouses, one for the boys and one for girls. A red-headed

Roza School, 1921.
Ellensburg Public Library

boy with freckles lived close to the Wenas area and rode by horseback to school. There was a small barn to take care of the horse.

The school had a cistern, which had been cleaned out nicely just before classes started. There were a lot of wild little creatures in there—frogs, mice, and once in a while a snake. We'd pull up a bucket of fresh water every morning and put it on a stand in the cloakroom with a dipper. The children helped themselves.

I had to fire up the stove in the morning. The big pot bellied stove burned coal and wood and had a big metal jacket around it. In wintertime, I'd stoke it at night, so the room wasn't too cold in the morning. I'd poke the coals a little bit and it would roar up again.

I was scheduled to teach 10 pupils. They came from three farm families and three other families whose fathers worked in the nearby silica mills. I don't believe I had any children from railroad worker families. One of the silica mills was operated by a Japanese family and another by a white family. Silica was mined in the hills east of the Yakima River and trucked to the bluffs across from Roza. It was dumped into tram cars, which were attached to cables running down across the river to the mills.

When classes began, I had one eighth grader, two seventh graders, one sixth, two fifth graders, a fourth, a third, and a little second grader. A little girl who was supposed to come for first grade would rather ride in the hills on her pony, with her dog running behind her, so she didn't start school that year. I had all those grades to manage and was kept busy figuring out how to do it.

School started when I rang the bell, and they came right in and took their seats. We started with the pledge of allegiance. I had assignments on the blackboard. All the ABCs, of course, were etched on top of the blackboard, so once in awhile I'd just get the pointer and we'd go through them, and sometimes sing the ABC song. I often combined classes, so I could teach longer lessons. For example, sometimes the third and fourth, or the fifth and sixth, could work together. The kids who wanted to be teacher's pet asked to clean

Roza silica mill and ore transport cables; looking west across the Yakima River.
Ellensburg Public Library

the erasers all the time. The students brought their own paper and pencils, but we didn't have a pencil sharpener. So Bynum "Barney" Roberts, the oldest student, had the job of sharpening pencils with a knife.

Mrs. Roberts told me I might have trouble, so I wanted to keep them under tow. Halloween naturally is a time for boys to act up. One of the boys got his feelings hurt. Others went with him in the evening and they soaped all the school's windows. When I saw the white marks on the window panes, I didn't say a word.

When Friday afternoon came, I said, "You kids have been so good and you've got your lessons all done and we're through. So I tell you what. We're going to have house cleaning. The girls and I will clean up inside and you boys go outside and wash the windows, and then we'll have a clean school-house for next Monday."

I didn't have to punish them severely; this was enough. They saw that they weren't getting away with soaping the windows. They had to clean up their own mess.

The school, of course, held plays and programs. One girl had a sweet voice; she could really sing! Anytime a program called for a song, she took the lead. Barney Roberts, the oldest boy and the son the of school clerk, was a good and smart student. I'd always give him something historical to recite. There was one little boy, Charlie; he was the cutest little fellow. I dressed him up as an old man one time and put him in the lead role for a play. He really brought down the house. He was a third grader and a clever little fellow, and so neat and clean with all of his books, papers, and everything. Then there was the freckle-faced redhead; he was a livewire, but I liked him. He wasn't a troublemaker, but I could see that he might've been.

At Christmas time, one of the boys brought a tree and I returned from home with a suitcase of Christmas trimmings so that the youngsters could decorate it. One of the parents played Santa Claus, and a few presents were passed between the children and myself. Santa Claus passed out popcorn and candy, and the students had a little exchange of gifts. The Valentine's Day party, on the other hand, was just for the students, with an exchange of valentines. They made their own cards, and learned about St. Valentine and how the holiday began.

One time that spring, they said, "You know, we have wild onions around here. Did you ever taste any?"

Of course I'd tasted farm grown onions, but I said, "Not wild ones exactly."

"We'll show you where you find them."

We went up on a hill just back of the schoolhouse, where wild onions grew out from under flat rocks several inches across. In picking up one of those flat rocks, there'd be about a half dozen little fresh onions. They tasted like onions, but were pretty strong.

I was a little afraid of rattlesnakes. I thought, "Oh, what if a snake would come out? What'll I do if it gets to a youngster when I'm not close by?" I'd been told there were a lot of snakes here in the springtime, but I never saw any. It was nice and sunny day and the snakes stayed away, thank goodness.

Also in the springtime, some of the boys played baseball during recess, but I warned them not to throw or hit a ball toward the schoolhouse. I didn't want any broken windows. The playground also had swings and teeter-totters for the kids. At Easter, I brought colored eggs from home and hid them outside around the school. It was nice and sunny weather, and after the second recess I let them go out and hunt for the eggs. They found them all, even those hidden in the craziest places.

It was all very inexpensive, the things we did in those days. A couple of community dances were held at the school. Following the lead of a fiddler, couples did two-steps or a waltz. Nothing fancy, but everyone had fun.

I only taught one year at Roza. The superintendent never did come to the school to observe my classroom. The only way to get down there was by train or handcar. There's nothing standing at Roza today. The silica mills and the little cabins for the working families are gone. Even the stone farmhouse where I lived has disappeared.

Dora Emerson Cissel tells a story about going to a dance at the Roza School in 1924. The only way to get to Roza at that time was by the railway. Her date put her on a hand car and pumped them to the school. He said not to worry about meeting a train along the way as he could easily stop and lift the hand car off the tracks. At the school, the children's desks were pushed out of the way to make room for dancing. A fiddler and an accordion player provided the music, and a good time was held by all.

A typical railway hand car.
Ellensburg Public Library

The next year I taught close to home at the Edgemont-Thrall School #36, on Number Six Road down behind Moe Hill. It was a typical rural school, but quite large. I had 20 pupils. I drove an old Ford to school from my parents' place close to Thrall. Along the way, I'd pick up about a half-dozen youngsters. I could put three in front and three in back, and that was about all the car could hold. I just drove the kids from our neighborhood, since they lived farthest from the school. In going to the schoolhouse early, they could help me out. They cleaned the blackboards and erasers if it hadn't been done the day before, and the bigger kids carried in water from the outside pump.

We had a bucket and dipper, and the students washed their hands in the cloakroom where they hung their clothes; it really was the only place where they could. The school had the typical barn, outhouses, swings, and teeter-totters. I used my hand bell here, too. Some of the pupils would ask to ring it, and if they'd been real good the last day or so, I'd give them the privilege. One day when playing baseball with the children, I fell on a rusty stovepipe and cut myself. I bled profusely and had to call the doctor.

A little side room had a heating element of some sort, and I might've been able to fix hot lunches. But I didn't bother with that. I was afraid one of the kids might get burned.

Students at the Edgemont-Thrall School, 1921. "Nell" is in the front row. Front row (l. to r.): Earl Sorenson, Marion Sorenson, Wilburt Sorenson, unknown, Bill Jensen, teacher Nellie Donald, Betty Phelps, Eloise Kay, and Frances Whitendale. Back row (l. to r.): Charles Blackman, Dan Waite, Ken Jefferies, Harold Ringer, Eugene Nole, Lillie Mae Simons, D.B. Jefferies, Bernice Tozer, Mildred Kay, Ruby Donald, Earlene Jensen, and Joan Sieble.
Helen "Nell" Donald Hadley

At this school, one gentleman, Mr. Jeffers, liked to participate in the programs and other events. He helped out and entertained us lots of times. Sometimes he'd dress up in an apron as an old washerwoman and sang ditties that made everyone laugh. Mrs. Sybil, an excellent pianist, also played for us a lot.

It was really difficult for me at the Edgemont-Thrall School because all the kids knew me. Our families were neighbors and had visited each others' homes and attended parties and dinners together. When I played with the kids at recess, they all called me Nellie. One day a mother told her first grader, "She's not Nellie today. She's not Nellie anymore. She's Miss Donald. Don't call her Nellie."

One little boy, who was so proud of himself, went home one day and said, "Mama, I didn't call her Nellie once!"

A sixth grade girl had an excellent voice and I depended on her for singing. I always gave her a big part in the programs. Some youngsters were good in art, so I'd let them help out. If the eighth grade girl had her work done, she'd go into the other little room and help some of the first graders with writing, ABCs, and things like that. I'd give her extra duties because she was smart and always finished her lessons. Those are the advantages of a rural school,

Mrs. Hadley, 1975.

but it's also a lot more work for the teacher to keep things organized. The superintendent visited the Edgemont-Thrall school, unlike at Roza, which was so remote.

Both school programs and neighborhood gatherings were held at the Edgemont-Thrall School. One high school girl came to the parties with a friend. They both sang while one of them played the guitar. We had some nice programs, and they weren't all school programs. A lot of the families sang together in those days.

7

I Always Wanted to Teach

Ruby Gustafson Haberman, 1925–30

I always wanted to teach. I don't know why, but I just did. I remember thinking one time that maybe I should be a nurse. Mother said, "Oh no, you wouldn't want to be a nurse. You will go to school." She knew that was what I always wished to do.

I wanted to start a career as soon as I could. It was after World War I and times were hard. I knew I had to get going and take care of myself.

I only have faint recollections of college. As soon as I finished high school, I began with summer school at the Normal School and completed two quarters. I took some primary work and some intermediate education classes. I do remember taking kindergarten work under Miss Meisner. The only instructor I remember particularly well was Professor Fish, an excellent professor who taught history.

I was 18 and one of those they pushed along pretty fast. They questioned whether I was old enough to receive a temporary teaching certificate. But since my birthday came along about the same time as I signed a contract, they let me have it. A lot of my girlfriends were looking for jobs too. We'd gone together and applied.

The first school I taught at was the same one I'd attended as a child, Lower Naneum. I think I received $110 a month. Nobody would advise you to teach in

Clara Meisner, kindergarten training school supervisor, 1906–38.
Ellensburg Public Library

your home district, but I lived out there, so I did. It was a small one room building and had bare wood floors, but the walls were painted. A big coal stove with a shield of some sort provided heating. There was a teacher's desk and a chair. The rows of students' desks were attached to long floor planks. You had to lift or slide the whole row to move them; this was quite a chore. I was the janitor, and "trying" to sweep underneath those desks was difficult.

Mounted on the walls was a Seth Thomas clock and pictures of George Washington and Abraham Lincoln, an old windmill scene, and a print of *The Gleaners.*[1] These were quite old and I believe they'd hung there when I was a student at the school. There were no electric lights, but the room had large windows on each side and sash curtains halfway up. There was a globe, chalk boards and erasers, and some roll-up maps that could be pulled down.

A teacher was fortunate if she could talk somebody out of a ball for use on the playground. I usually had to buy them. The boys brought their baseball bats, if they had them, or we'd use a stick or whatever for playing games. There wasn't much other equipment. The students brought their own books and supplies, which was expensive for families. When I was in school, it was quite a worry for my father to buy books for his four children. The students walked to school or rode horses, or sometimes came in a buggy carrying three or four children.

The first year, I taught 29 students in grades one through eight. I was 18 and had a 16-year-old repeating the eighth grade. In those days, students needed to pass a state exam to earn an eighth grade certificate. Evidently, he hadn't passed a subject or two. I now realize he was disappointed at being there. He was unhappy and surly. I could've had a great deal more trouble with him, but somehow I didn't.

Students met in rooms at the county superintendent's office for the eighth grade examination. It was quite an awesome thing. My brother and I took it when we were at the same school. A student was tested in various subjects. In Physiology, I had to name bones, joints, and muscles. I'm sure the children I later had would've failed. We also were tested in Agriculture, a subject taught to eighth graders at the time. It was difficult for some students because they didn't have any experience with farming or animals. Fortunately for me, my father farmed and raised horses, cows, pigs, and sheep.

Programs were the highlight of the school year. Teachers were expected to prepare them at Christmas, Halloween, and in the springtime. Toward the end of the school year, I had my students put on a circus, held outside. The children built cages for their "wild animals"—cats, dogs, and chickens—and we had a Maypole.

Mothers always helped out by providing food and treats. We all had a good time. School picnics also were held at the end of the year. The children and their families usually gathered in one of the nearby canyons for a day. Homemade ice cream, chicken, and potato salad were three of the mainstays.

When the weather was warm, I'd take my students out to pick wildflowers. Back at the school, we'd classify, press, and sketch the flowers. We collected frog eggs in the spring and observed them for awhile. We did a lot of these things, which were my particular interest. I even collected snake skins and garter snakes; we had a lot of fun with that, of course.

I recall that the only time the school closed was during a dust storm coming in from the east. The storm blew by Kittitas leaving an inch or more of dirt everywhere. The school remained closed for a day or two until the dust settled and the school was cleaned up.

After two years at Lower Naneum (1925–27), I next taught at the Woldale School (1927–29). It was much the same as the other small schools, but a little nicer, with lighting, more books, newer maps and pictures, and generally more things to work with. The children again were much the same—very lovely really, for the most part. However, I always seemed to have one little guy with problems he couldn't get over or caused by things he really wasn't responsible for.

I worked at Woldale two years, and then went to the town of Selah way down the Yakima River. I loved that school. It was a nice job teaching second grade, but traveling that far worried my father. I commuted with three others from the Kittitas Valley who taught in the Selah schools at the time. We took turns driving each week. Two of them smoked, but they only had time for two cigarettes before we were either in Selah or back home—that was the way I could handle it. It was an interesting and fun time being with people sharing the same interests.

The county superintendent came to visit the school two or three times. The children were more aware of the superintendent's importance than I was, I think. It didn't seem to worry me any. I also attended the Teachers Institute, which had a speaker and music. The main event, as far as I was concerned, was going out to lunch with some friends. I'm afraid I looked on it as a kind of vacation. I don't think the institutes ever helped particularly.

I lived in our family home during the years I taught in rural schools—my folks were farmers, and I walked or commuted to school. Most rural teachers, of course, resided with a local family and worked or paid for their board. I knew a teacher who drove the family's horse to school, taking their two children. She also washed the supper dishes to earn her board.

Some of the parents had attended high school and even college, but most had a grade school education and probably not much beyond the fifth grade. The parents of some of my foreign children were schooled in Switzerland and probably had a reasonably good education, as my folks did. I didn't have any pupils who couldn't speak and understand English; I think it was spoken in all their homes. My mother had finished high school in Norway and for the standards of those days she had a good education. She taught herself English here; she could read and write, and correct us, though she never lost her Norwegian accent.

I don't know if the community's attitude toward me was typical or not. I think they just figured I was part of the community and they took me for better or worse. They were very kind to me. I'm sure I couldn't have been treated better. A lot of this was due to my folks; I'm sure of that, because they, too, were that type of people. I don't believe the parents gave the school's curriculum much thought. They expected the children to learn and to make progress—basically asking not much more than "could they read?" But they always did everything that I asked of them.

Children in the rural schools and the city schools were the same—they were lovely. You have the good ones and the mischievous ones and the brilliant ones and the slow ones. However, I liked the companionship in the city schools, where I had teachers to talk to and discuss things. When you were alone teaching in a rural school, everything was on your shoulders. You had to handle all the discipline, for example. It took me awhile in the city schools to start relying on the principal in this regard. Initially for me, going for the principal's help was a sign of failure—I couldn't handle my own room.

In the city schools, when teaching only at one level, say fifth grade, the children still had different skills somewhat similar to a rural school where you taught all the grades. In a city school's fifth grade class, some of the pupils might be reading only at a third or fourth grade level, while others were advanced and even reading up to an eighth grade standard. You still had this kind of variation no matter where you taught.

Rural schools, of course, had some limitations for the students. They didn't have much opportunity to meet new boys and girls, and they didn't have much access to libraries and books like city kids, or some other facilities. We sometimes held basket socials to raise money to buy books. It was really something special when a box of books arrived. The postman would drop it off at the door, and I'd dismiss classes for the day and go through the books. But overall, children in rural schools did just fine, particularly in regard to the context of those times. The city schools, too, back then didn't have the range of facilities and opportunities like modern schools. You've got to take it all in perspective.

Note

1. *The Gleaners* (*Des glaneuses*) is a well-known oil painting by French artist Jean-François Millet showing three peasant women picking up stray wheat grains in a field after harvest. Completed in 1857, it became famous in Europe and the United States for memorializing the hard-laboring lower classes of society.

8

No Woman Teach My Boys

THERESA MUS McKNIGHT, 1925-27

Theresa was 93 at the time of this interview in June 1999.

When I was in high school, I wanted to become a lawyer. Miss Merchant, the principal, called me into the office and said she'd heard about my intentions. She said, "People don't have faith in women lawyers, I think you should be a teacher." This wouldn't be the only time that people pushed me toward being a teacher.

I couldn't afford to go to a big college away from home and study to be a lawyer. I was lucky I could go to the Normal School in Ellensburg! I was 16 when graduating as salutatorian from Cle Elum High School in 1923. Right away that fall, I went to the Normal School. I still wanted to go to a bigger college, but my cousins said to my father, "Don't let her change her mind. If she gets some work done here, it's a good start." See, I didn't have a mother; she died when I was nine years old.

My dad replied, "That will be a good start, so that's where she's going."

When I talked to a woman professor, she said, "You're doing alright. You stay right with it here at the Normal School."

So I became a teacher. I'm not sorry I taught school. I think about it in this way: What would I do if I had to make a choice again? Am I sorry I did this or that? No, I'd make the same choice: I'd teach school.

After completing two years at college, I applied to several places for a job all the next year without getting anything. Finally, I don't know how in the world it ever happened, but I was hired at the Ballard School out in the country in northern Kittitas County.

I taught at Ballard from 1925 to 1927 and remember starting at $115 a month, and $125 the second year. Oh, I enjoyed it so much! I'd go back and do it again. The first day was hard, though, because I wasn't sure of myself and wasn't sure of the kids. I'd never attended a one-room rural school like that myself. Well, these kids kept coming in and coming in, and I sat them down in this row and that row, until I finally got the kids all seated. I had quite a big roomful of students. I was beginning to get them all lined up when I heard loud footsteps coming up the porch.

I went to the outer door and there stood this strange man, glaring at me. He said, "I come here! I say no! No woman teach my boys! You a woman and I say no woman teach my boys!"

I told him who I was, what I was doing, where I came from, and all that. We talked for over an hour. The kids were very quiet. When finally leaving, he said, "I tell school board before, 'No woman teach my kids!'"

Well, I think there were five country schools up there when I started and none of them had a male teacher. He was crazy anyway and that was the only time I saw him. He left his boys in school and I never had any trouble with them. The second year, though, he didn't send his kids to me. They went to a neighboring school, taught by a woman teacher who was a friend of mine. Not long afterwards, the middle boy—I can still see him now—didn't come home. They found him up on the mountain—he'd shot himself. That little boy killed himself. It was a terrible, terrible thing, but there wasn't anything we could do.

All the classes sat together in the Ballard School's one big room. Off to the side there were a couple of little rooms, with one serving as a kind of kitchenette. We didn't have a pump and well, so we had to haul water. The school stood half way up a hill from a pond that was the source of our drinking

Theresa Mus and her students at the Ballard School, 1927.
Ellensburg Public Library

water. The kids took turns bringing up buckets of water. We had a dipper, but no one drank from it; they had their own cups. The students brought their lunches and nobody went home at noon.

During the first month, I didn't need to heat the room because the weather was warm. When chilly days finally arrived, I started the furnace for a couple of months and then I'd had enough. I hired Charlie, a responsible eighth grader, to do it for me. He didn't live far from the school, maybe a good half mile, and he could come early and start the furnace to warm up the room. The big furnace stood in the basement and there was only one outlet in the floor to allow heat to come up. During the winter when the children came into the school, they'd stand around that large round grate to get warm, but I wouldn't let them put their shoes on it; the heat would damage their footwear. I'd put a big kettle of milk on the grate so everybody could have hot chocolate with their lunches.

One day, the little stove in the kitchenette caught fire. I grabbed that stove and threw it as far into the school yard as I could and it burst into flames. I later told the school board, "I don't want a stove. I don't want it anymore." That's when we started using the furnace grate to warm up milk for hot chocolate.

In those days, teachers had detailed directives and programs to guide them in teaching each of the classes. Teachers also could give spankings. I always had a paddle, but never had much trouble.

There were strong family-teacher relationships in the Ballard District that you didn't see in town. The teacher was expected to stay overnight in each of the family homes once a year, getting to know the parents and dining with them. It was the first time I ever ate cooked dandelion. We'd always eaten raw dandelion at home, and I loved dandelion with oil and vinegar and hard-boiled eggs; my dad always fixed that. This time I had cooked dandelion! When I stayed with the Carollo family—they had nine kids in school—all the children clamored over who'd be the one to sleep next to the teacher. Oh, that was really something.

I walked two miles to school. The kids walked, too, from their homes. During periods of bad weather, Mr. Carollo fixed up the back of his truck for hauling his children and other kids. We called it the "Teanaway Bus." He put hay on the floor to help keep them warm and the panels of the truck blocked the wind. Now when I think about it: That was dangerous! A spark could've started a fire and burned all those kids up! Why didn't we think about that back then? It doesn't make sense to me now.

In those days, teachers were so concerned about their kids! We tried to make a difference in young people's lives. A girl in my school was turning 16, the age at which a student could quit school. She came up to me saying, "You know, tomorrow is my last day of school."

I was just shocked. I replied, "Marion! Why?"

"I'll be 16 years old tomorrow and I don't have to go to school anymore."

Oh, that killed me. She was an orphan and living with relatives on a farm two miles away. It was a cold day in December, so I got a ride on the "Teanaway Bus"—the only time I rode it—and went out to their farm.

After I arrived, they said, "Now, it's up to Marion whether she wants to go back to school or not." I put in my two bits worth and asked her not to quit. "Marion you can do better. You'll be 16 and I told you before that I'd get you through the seventh grade test and the eighth grade test in one year, the two of them. Then you'll have that behind you."

I talked and talked, but didn't get anywhere. Finally, after her 16th birthday, she quit. Later she lived in California, and now and then came to see me when visiting our area.

The school stood on the middle of Ballard Hill, with half the kids living above the school and half below. It was great place for sledding. During one recess when I was out playing in the snow with the kids, one of the girls offered to let me use her sled. The kids started clamoring for the teacher to ride the sled down the hill. I carried the sled up to the main road by the school and lay down flat on it. The girl flopped on top of me and off we went. Boy, were we going! When we came to a little curve on Ballard Hill and made a slight turn, I suddenly flew in one direction and she in the other. I landed on my stomach. Oh! It knocked the wind out of me. We piled up at the foot of the hill. I was about to die and she was laughing her head off. She thought it was funny. And me—I thought, "Oh! I hope I've survived this one!" She was little and light, but I'd hit hard; I tell you I felt it. But anyway, we survived that episode.

No local Indian children attended my school, but Indian families did come around now and then. One morning when coming to school, I saw an old truck parked in the school barn. I thought, "Golly! Who would have a truck like that around here?" It turned out that a group of Indians had spent the night in the barn. I was a little fearful, but they were friendly. The Indians and the local people always got along well.

When I was a youngster, every fall we'd go up into the Cascade Mountains to pick huckleberries, just as the regional Indians were accustomed to doing.

At least one of our mothers would go with us. We usually caught a passenger train at about 2 a.m. in Cle Elum. Sometimes we rode freight trains.

One time when climbing into a freight car, I heard voices in the dark. A whole lot of bums were sitting around in there. We sat there with them. We weren't scared; not one bit. On top of that we were all girls and they were very nice to us. At the summit, the engineer stopped and let us off. Then the train continued through the summit tunnel on its way to Puget Sound. We had a train schedule and knew when we needed to get back to the station the next day and catch a ride back to Cle Elum. The engineer, aware that he had a bunch of youngsters aboard, always was very careful with us.

We then went five miles up the mountain along a creek to the place where we picked berries and camped by a lake. We went up there every year. This time we saw a tent right by the lake, and pretty soon a forest ranger came up, saying, "You can use my tent. I'm going down back home so I won't need it tonight." We were glad, the chaperones too, because we'd always slept out in the open.

Indians also were camped around the lake. You know, we were crazy kids. All night long we laughed and giggled and talked in the tent. We didn't sleep much. One Indian lady in the first tent next to us wasn't happy about it. She said, "Heap much noise." And kept saying again, "Heap much noise!" It was the truth. They wanted and needed to sleep because they were in the business of picking berries. And here we were, making all kinds of noise. But we finally fell asleep.

The next day we needed to wash up a bit, but didn't have soap. I don't know how they got me to go ask for soap from the Indian lady, but they did. They gave me 10¢ and said, "You go tell her you want some soap." The Indian lady didn't understand me. So I went over to her little girl, who had dirt on her little face, and I made washing motions. The Indian lady broke out in a smile. She knew right away, and turned around and got a sliver of soap from her tent. I tried to give her the dime, but she wouldn't take it, so I gave it to the little girl.

One time after teaching all day, I started out late toward the home where I boarded, which stood about two miles away. It was getting dark. I was little afraid because it was after we'd found people sleeping in the school barn. I started up the long hill in the dark. I'd forgotten how close by the cemetery was, and halfway up the hill I really got the jitters. I thought to myself, "You've got to go by there!" I saw a light in this house where a lady and her daughter lived. I thought, "Maybe I'll just stop there for a minute."

Just then, I heard a car trying to make it up the hill with its motor working hard. (Years ago around there, if someone bought a car and wanted to be sure it was a good one, they'd try it out on Ballard Hill. If you could get up that hill with no problem, it was a good car.) So I heard this automobile coming up the hill…chug-chug-chug. It slowed down in front of the farmhouse. The people in the car were out looking for me; they were from the family I boarded with.

The Cle Elum school superintendent had told me that after I got some experience—which meant teaching in a small school for two years—he'd have a job for me. He kept his word. After I taught at Ballard for two years, my contract came in the mail. I was surprised because I hadn't seen him in a couple of years.

That fall, I began teaching at the Hazelwood Elementary School in Cle Elum. The funny thing was, I'd gone to school there for eight years, and got many "lickin's" in the third grade for talking out of turn. I ended up teaching in that very same third grade room! I've never regretted my decision to teach. I'd do it all over again if I could.

On April 17, 1975, the *Northern Kittitas County Tribune* in Cle Elum ran a short article about Mrs. McKnight's teaching experiences at the Ballard School. It was titled "Another Story," and written by Peter Fassero in a series on "Upper County One Room Schools"—

In the fall…Miss Theresa Mus applied for and got the job at Ballard School. Her salary: $115 a month on a nine month basis…

She was paid this magnificent sum for teaching, acting as janitor, cook (hot chocolate at noon for the kids), and carrying drinking water from the creek at the bottom of Ballard Hill.

It was considered a prize job because of its size, averaging 26 pupils from the first grade through the eighth. I forgot—she acted as school nurse too, because there were no phones or buses in those days to rely on.

Heating the school was a problem. Miss Mus partially solved it by hiring young Charles Bonaudi (8th grade boy) to start the fire each school day. She paid him $5 a month. His folks lived near the school…

There were several rural schools within a radius of 10 miles: Ballard, with Mrs. Theresa (Mus) McKnight—Virden, with Mary (Padavich) Eaton—Liberty School, with Luch Eaden—and the Bristol School, with Theresa (Bugni) Bettas as teacher.

Mrs. McKnight said it was a customary practice for the teachers to participate in all social events in the community. Consequently, every two to four weeks, a program would be held at each school on a rotating basis.

The programs began late, as the farmers had to do their chores first. The children would present a school program at the beginning, followed by games and dancing to the accordion music of Louis Bonino—until the wee hours of the morning. This completed the evening's entertainment.

The popular dances of the '20s were circle two steps, old fashioned waltzes and fox trots. Polkas, ladies tags, men's tags and marathon dances were also on the agenda. The tune most requested was the "Beer Barrel Polka."

Pie socials, box socials, etc. were usually held on Saturday nights with food furnished by the participating school. Ballard school was the popular choice because the size of the building, the stage and the kitchen were the largest. Midnight lunch consisted of sandwiches, cookies, cake or pie with plenty of coffee.

Most of the pupils walked to school—including the nine Carollo children who traveled 3½ miles each way. Speaking of the Carollos—all nine of them—Isabel, Tony, Alice, Julia, Quinto, Albina, Albeno, Pete and Peggy—were taught by Mrs. McKnight. Theresa said, "Teaching them was no problem. They were well-behaved youngsters."

The Evans' girl rode to school on horseback, coming all the way from beyond the present Hidden Valley Ranch. The Emericks came from Lookout Mountain. There was a large barn at the foot of Ballard Hill for the horses…

Tony Carollo was hired by the school board to drive the children to school during the winter months. He used a team of horses hitched to a sled with a canvas covering—like a covered wagon [*Theresa remembered Carollo using a truck; perhaps at another time?*]. Two benches, one on each side of the sled, a straw covered floor, plus a lighted kerosene stove in the center—completed the picture. It was a miracle no fires or accidents resulted.

When nice weather prevailed, Theresa would often drive the kids home in her Model T Ford with a rumble seat. Believe it or not, she would stuff twelve youngsters into that Ford!

Mrs. McKnight boarded and roomed at the Alfred Hansons' home during the years she taught at Ballard School. It was customary for the teacher to have dinner and stay overnight with each family once during the school year. The girls in each family would argue and fight for the privilege of sleeping with the teacher.

Walking to and from Hansons to school during the winter months was a hardship—sometimes wading through snow drifts up to her waist. "Two miles seemed ever so long a distance," she said.

During 1926 the main cross-state highway between Spokane and Seattle wound past the Ballard School. Many a morning Theresa would walk [*two miles along the highway*] to school without meeting a single highway traveler.

One of her most scary experiences was driving home to Cle Elum from school one Friday evening. It was a wintry night and as she started out, the lights on her Ford went out while driving on the main highway. She managed to keep the wheels in the two ruts, then followed the ruts all the way to town, ten miles away. Fortunately, she didn't meet another car…

Theresa…I recall a compliment the late Vernon Peterson, former editor of the *Miner Echo*, paid you. He said you were the best English teacher he ever had!

9

Where Is That Teacher

MARY HARTMAN GUSTAFSON, 1925–27

Mrs. Gustafson was 94 when I interviewed her at the Monterey Gardens apart-
ments in Ellensburg. She had recently sold her home; it was too much for her to
keep up. She was playing solitaire when I came in, handling the cards with rapid
precision. She was a small woman who eyed me with pert attention and a no non-
sense bearing. She straightened me out right at the beginning, putting her cards
aside and saying, "Don't call it an interview—just say, 'she talked.'"

I got my first job by applying for it; simply that. I'd taken
two years of Normal School. You could teach with one
year, but I earned a two year teaching certificate. I just
applied and the board granted me a job.

When I began working, I taught at the Lyons School
#14 on the Lyons Road just north of Kittitas. It also was
called Woodpecker College. I don't know why it had that
name; it just did.[1] In those days, life was so simple and if
somebody said something like that, it stuck and nobody questioned it.

The first year, I boarded with an elderly woman who had a son and
daughter, both middle-aged and unmarried. Her little house stood about a
mile from the school and I walked all the time, either up the road or through
a field. The second year, I boarded in the Pete Edmonds home, which was
located only about a block or so from the schoolhouse on the same road.

I received $125 a month. Some of the smaller schools paid $120, but
$125 was about standard for a country school, which seemed like a lot of
money to me. I paid $25 for room and board, so I cleared $100 a month,
and for eight months, $800. I returned to college in the summertime, finish-
ing up my third year, and still had $1,000 left. I divided it with my sister.
We attended the state college in Pullman for our senior year on that $1,000,
boarding together in the same room.

The Lyons School was a one room building with large windows along the
sides. Inside, there were rows of attached desks for the pupils, and a black-

board extended across the room behind the teacher's desk. Underneath each desktop, there was a little storage shelf where the students put their books and supplies. There also was a globe, and large pull down maps on rollers of Europe and the United States. Two little anterooms in back served as the library and the girls' cloakroom. The boys' cloakroom was behind the front porch. In wintertime, students came in all bundled up and had to store their coats and scarves someplace. Those living the farthest away rode by horseback; we had a little barn in back for the animals. A couple of outhouses also stood out back—one for the boys and one for girls.

A little room for a kitchen had been built on to the back of the building. Around 1915 or so, the school districts got the idea that children should have hot lunches. Little kitchens were added and provided with some kind of stove to cook on. We mostly served soup, macaroni and cheese, baked beans, cocoa, and other foods that could easily be warmed up. I'd get lunch started and assign a seventh grader to watch it, keeping the food from burning, and then to serve it.

I personally didn't fire up the main stove to heat the room. I'd hire an eighth grade boy to come an hour early and start it. I also hired a boy to do the janitorial work every night after school.

I taught about 32 children in all eight grades. The kids begin arriving around 8:30 a.m. In wintertime, when the days were short, I always ended classes a little earlier; we'd take only a half hour off at noon, instead of an hour. At the end of the day, this allowed the children to leave a half hour early to get home, and some had far to go. It was the custom here. In the worst weather, parents often brought their children in the morning, particularly the smallest ones, and also picked them up. Sometimes so much snow fell that I couldn't let the little kids go out for recess; the directors said to keep them in. During the half hour at noon, I had them do calisthenics at their desks instead of going out to play.

The day started when I rang the bell. The kids lined up, marched in, and took their seats. We usually saluted the flag and then went to work. I started with the youngest pupils, such as in first grade reading. I always did this initially because the younger ones needed more time for presentation than the older students. Then I went through the grades on a schedule—reading and arithmetic, geography and history, and so forth for all the grades. I also taught art and music. A teacher had to maintain a tight schedule. I'd arrange it so that the smaller children came first and the older children last. This not only was good for the smaller children, but gave the older pupils—with more lessons—sufficient time to prepare.

I learned to combine classes, such as second and third grade reading, or music and art. I'd give them a set of questions to do, and then check the results before recess or before a period ended. I'd give them another group of questions for the next day. I didn't have so many papers to carry home and check because the classes were small, with only several pupils in each grade level. I checked their work, but didn't necessarily assign a graded score every time. I well knew how my children were progressing by working closely with them everyday.

Report cards came out monthly, with every subject listed and graded. Deportment, too, was graded—regarding how well behaved and cooperative they were. The older students received numbered grades—90s were good, 80s about average, and 70s might mean improvement was needed.

Outside during recess, they played "Pom-pom-pullaway." Two teams were formed, one on each side of the schoolhouse. One group threw a ball over the roof hollering, "Pom-pom-pullaway, let your horses run away." The team on the other side scrambled to catch it; and if they did, they called out in the same way when returning the ball over the building. They also played tag, hide and seek, and I suppose just what kids have done forever.

It wasn't the custom to play baseball in the fall. But in the spring, boy, it was baseball all the time. One of the boys would bring a ball from home and I had to participate! I always was present on the playground, usually getting the little kids started in playing something. But in the spring, when those bigger boys played baseball, I had to play, too. I couldn't be the pitcher because I couldn't throw, I couldn't be the catcher because I couldn't catch, and I couldn't bat very well either, but they didn't seem to mind that. I was young then—being 20, 21, 22 years old. I think kids going to a rural school appreciated having a young teacher able to participate in their fun.

A county superintendent came twice a year to see if the students were up to standards. The superintendent observed a teacher's preparation, methods, and how well subjects were being taught and what the children were getting out of it. The superintendent also reviewed exams taken by the students. While observing whether the pupils were up to par, the superintendent actually was judging a teacher's competence and ability.

One spring, just as the superintendent arrived, we were all out playing baseball when one of the boys got hit. I was over there with that kid on the baseball field, trying to assure him and seeing if he needed any medical care, when I saw the superintendent drive up. She went inside and couldn't find me. I didn't go in, but stayed with the hurt boy. She came out the other side of the building to where the little kids were playing and loudly proclaimed, "Where is that teacher?"

It was funny about those kids that time. Kids are kids, and once in a while they'll smirk and smart off behind your back, but when she watched us that afternoon I had the perfect classroom. They worked, they studied, they answered questions, and they raised their hands. You'd thought they acted that way always. Well, they did almost, but this time they really laid it on.

The eighth graders had to take the state examinations at the county superintendent's office. In my first year of teaching, I had some boys who were a little older than they should've been—like 14 and 16 years old. They were allowed to take the eighth grade test at Christmas time because they were older. Two of them passed, placing first and third in the state! They were exceptionally smart boys, and one of them went on to teach. I don't think the exams were particularly hard. I think anybody could've done any amount of work, even minimal, and pass.[2]

I didn't have any discipline problems when I taught. Even when I was a child going to grade school, I only observed one disciplinary problem in all that time. As a child, I first attended the Lower Naneum School #20, and then went to the Rolinger School #31, which stood where the Ellensburg airport now is located. I remember the girl who had the disciplinary problem— she was big girl and appeared older than her actual age. I don't know what the difficulty was, but she decided she was going home. She packed up her books and was ready to go. The teacher, who was much smaller than that big girl, just went over to the door and stood there. She told her to go back and sit

Mary Hartman (front row, sixth from left) as a student at the Rolinger School, District #31.
Ellensburg Public Library

down, and the girl finally did. She was a good teacher by the way. That's the only time I remember any insubordination at all.

In those days, a teacher in a rural community had much the same status as a minister or doctor. If a student had a fever or upset stomach, I'd phone the parents and tell them to come and get them. We had a county nurse, but you didn't call her. She only came to visit once in a while to see if the school's hygiene practices were alright. Getting inoculations were up to the parents, but nobody did it. It was something that didn't have its day yet.

We held Christmas, Mayday, and other programs, usually in the evenings with all the parents present. Sometimes a box social preceded the program. It was fun. The students were able to show off their literary and language skills with little short skits and speaking a piece, and some might sing or play an instrument. The kids were wonderful and loved it. They would've held a program every Friday if I'd let them. Life was much simpler then; there weren't many social activities and expectations for it weren't high, but every parent came and they were proud of what their child did.

Baseball, a favorite springtime sport, ca. 1920.
Ellensburg Public Library

During the Christmas season, I had a tree if somebody provided one. People were poor by today's standards. A child was fortunate in getting one gift at home, and lucky to get a small present from the teacher. But Christmas was Christmas and it was an exciting time; fun was had with little expense.

During my first year of teaching, my walk to school was about a mile along the road, but somewhat less through a field, so I usually cut through the field. I remember one time in winter when I'd stayed a little late at the school. It was getting dark and fog came in over the snow as I set out toward the house where I boarded. I couldn't see where I was going. I knew that if I went straight to my right till I came to a fence, I then could follow the fence down to the barnyard. I had reached that fence and was about halfway down when I met the people I boarded with. They'd been up and down the road in a car looking for me, and were starting to search on foot when they found me.

People had automobiles in those days, but didn't use them too frequently to go places like today. Families were lucky to visit town just several times a year for shopping and to meet other people. Someone new and young—a teacher—coming to a rural neighborhood was really something to the kids, and they were so nice to me. To the parents, too, you weren't just "a teacher," but "the teacher!" In those days it was quite the thing.

Who named the schools in those days? It was the people living in those localities who dubbed them. Then in the 1930s or early 1940s, rural districts were consolidated into the Ellensburg District and most of those country schools were closed. The rural schools were special. The students liked each other, played with each other, and were nice to each other. If they played tricks on one another, it was like Halloween stunts—they let you know it was for fun and everybody laughed. It was done with goodwill, never with malice.

In the country there really weren't many children around. If youngsters happened to live next door to each other, they were good friends. But where families lived miles apart, as many did, children from different homes only saw each other occasionally, other than at school. So it was harder to see friends, but also harder to make enemies. Each family was more of a distinct social unit in those times. When I was child, if we got a friend to come to our house once a year, we were lucky. And there was only one girl near enough to come. But in those days, "life was real, life was earnest," and to me it was fun.

Notes

1. See Chapter 2 for the origin of the name "Woodpecker College."
2. Look at the eighth grade exams in the Appendix and see if you agree!

10

Howdy Schoolmarm

VERNA BOEDCHER WATSON, 1925–27

Mrs. Watson was 90 when I interviewed her in Ellensburg in 1998. Her daughter, Barbara Brooks, shared parts of a life story her mother had written about her childhood and schoolgirl days. I've started with sections from Mrs. Watson's own written account of those years as they relate to her subsequent teaching career.

I was born April 5, 1907, in Peoh Point, a rural community about three miles south of Cle Elum. I had a brother, Adolph, who was two years older.

We attended the Peoh Point School #40, located about five miles from our home. The school had what we called the little room and the big room. Grades one to four were taught in the little room, and five to eight in the big room. There was a playroom, too, with a stage at one end for school performances and eighth grade graduation exercises. The schoolhouse was the social center of the community. Children were transported to school in a horse drawn wagon during the fall and spring, and by sled in the winter. Straw and hot rocks were used to keep our feet relatively warm.

Peoh Point School, ca. 1914.
Ellensburg Public Library

Peoh Point school wagon.
Ellensburg Public Library

At the close of the eighth grade, we were required to pass the Washington State examinations, if we were to graduate. The state continued giving the test into the 1930s. There were four of us graduating in May 1920. We were very fortunate to have had Leta May Smith as our teacher that year. She made everything so interesting, though she was very thorough, too. Wild serviceberry bushes were in full bloom at the time. We created a bower of the white blossoms on our stage, under which we sat for the graduation exercises and received our certificates.

I was the only one in my class to attend high school. Traveling the three miles to Cle Elum posed a problem at first, but finally it was decided that I'd ride to school on our horse, Faithful Bob. I stabled him in a small barn close to the school. I needed to take a change of clothes each day. I don't know why I didn't find a place at school to store clothes, but I guess my folks decided for me. Riding horseback wasn't too bad during the fall and spring, but was most unpleasant during the cold winter months. I suffered in agony from cold feet and chilblains.

Living so far away, rarely could I take part in school activities. I developed some lasting friendships, however, chief among them being Virginia Cappellitti and her family. I sometimes was permitted to stay overnight with Virginia, and when I was chosen to take part in an operetta during my senior year, I stayed several days with Virginia's family so I could attend practices. That was probably the highlight of my high school career, except, of course, my graduation in May 1924. There were 37 of us in the class. Hugh Coleman was our superintendent, a big, shambling sort of man, liked and respected by everyone.

Even though I didn't take part in many activities in high school, I was involved in things in my community. I was a member of the 4H Club for several years, learning canning, cooking, sewing, and meal preparation, and I served as an assistant leader my last two years. The young people in our community held parties in various homes. One time when I was about 14, the local kids came and gave me a surprise birthday party. The next day I broke out with the measles, so I had exposed everybody. We held picnics in summer, sledded

Verna riding her horse to high school.
Barbara Brooks

in winter, and climbed nearby Peoh Point several times.

There was plenty of work to be done on the farm. Much of our livelihood depended on selling the produce we raised—fruit from our orchard and berry patches, vegetables from our large gardens, eggs from the large flocks of chickens, and milk, butter, and meat. When my brother died in the 1918 flu epidemic, I was the only child left to help with all the work and chores. I assisted with summertime haying, gathering potatoes, picking fruit and berries, weeding and thinning rows and rows of vegetables (for which I was paid 1¢ per row), cleaning barns, and tending to cows, calves, and pigs.

To earn extra money, my father served as the foreman of a construction crew making road improvements in our locality. The crew worked a 10 hour day. At those times, I was responsible in the evening for cleaning the cow barn, getting the cows into their stalls, and feeding them. Then my mother and I milked the cows, usually six or seven of them, and I separated the milk. I also fed the pigs and calves. When my father was home, he took the lead and I helped out. I thought an awful lot was expected of me, since no other girls my age were expected to do these chores. But then, there were boys to help out in other families.

My father was strict and I'm sure he had to be with "the likes of me." I was pretty headstrong, but I learned values and responsibility. In my leisure time, I'd read anything I got my hands on. My father was an avid reader, too, so there were lots of books, magazines, and newspapers in our house. My bedroom was upstairs and I carried a kerosene lamp to light my way up there. I'd sneak a book to my room before bedtime, and sometimes read till the wee hours.

I was just 17 when I graduated from Cle Elum High School in 1924. My father decided I should study to be a teacher. I entered the Normal School in Ellensburg that autumn and lived in Kamola Hall. I shared a room with Mary Padavich, a former schoolmate at Cle Elum High School. In those days, the house mother inspected our rooms at regular intervals, and, as part of our training, each of us was expected to take turns being a table hostess during the evening meals.

At the end of that year, I was allowed to teach for a couple of years. I applied at two schools: Nelson Siding #47 located between Cle Elum and Easton, and Dysart #5, east of Ellensburg. I was accepted by both, but took the one near Ellensburg because I thought I'd have a chance to meet more people. I would receive $125 a month for the nine month school year.

The Dysart School stood at the Naneum and Watson roads intersection. Dysart was a one room building, and quite a contrast to the Peoh Point School with its two rooms, stage, and indoor bathrooms. Indeed, the Peoh Point School was unusual for the times. Dysart, on the other hand, looked pretty small to me—and to think that I'd be teaching all those grades in it, too.

The school's facilities were as limited as could be. A big black stove burned wood and coal, and I was responsible for getting the fire going each morning, as well as cleaning the room at day's end. Fuel was stored in a little shed in back, and there were outhouses for the boys and the girls. There was a cloakroom where the kids could hang their coats, change boots, and so on. A bucket of water stood on a shelf; water had to be pumped by hand at the well. The desks were bolted in rows to footboards and the seats were hinged to turn up and down. The district furnished books, a dictionary, and encyclopedias, but the children had to bring their own paper, pencils, and crayons.

I taught from 1925 to 1927, and, of course, I had to arrange for room and board. My parents knew the Chris Christensens, who resided in the locality. They agreed that I could stay at their place for $25 a month. I walked about a mile between the house and school each day.

Of course, my legs were shaky that first day in the classroom. I thought, "Oh man, I've now signed myself up for this job and I'm going to have to do the best I can, as my father told me." A publication by the Washington State School Association stated the aims for students in each grade and what they should accomplish by the end of a nine month session. This provided goals for teachers and guided my curriculum. I was certainly glad to have it, knowing where to begin and where to end. I used it always.

Dysart school children.
Verna Boedcher Watson

School started and I don't remember having any troubles at all. I guess the students were as curious about me as I was about them. Anyway, we managed quite well. I do remember that the older students were good about helping out the little ones in their coursework. That was wonderful. As the months went by, I never had any parents come to me with complaints or objections, so I guess we did quite well.

The ringing of a big bell atop the building announced the start of school. I had around 20 or so children that first year in all the grades. While gazing toward the American flag, we began with the Pledge of Allegiance, and then sang several songs, such as "America" and "The Star Spangled Banner." The school didn't have a piano, so I'd just sing along with them; luckily, I could carry a tune.

I'd start with the little ones first, to get them going on things, and then proceed to the other grades throughout the day. I prepared a schedule beforehand so I'd know what needed to be done and how many minutes could be devoted to each subject, and to make sure that I got to everyone during the day. Of course, our studies more or less followed along with the provided textbooks. I often wrote on the chalkboard—there were two of them as I recall. I'd write questions and comments on the blackboard and have them respond or give answers. That's the way we did it in those times.

During recess, they played with a ball most of the time. I remember they threw the ball over the roof of the building while hollering "Pom-pom-pullaway, let your horses run away!" Students on the other side would try to catch the ball, and then throw it back. I'd ring a little bell to call them back inside.

Art had to be quite simple—mostly coloring, cutting and pasting, and once in a while painting. We used paint boxes with little watercolor blocks in them. We did simple things with watercolors, but had to be sure plenty of water was on hand to wash and cleanup afterward, and that was a little difficult. We made decorations for Halloween, and cards for the students' Valentine's Day boxes. The kids mostly made the valentine cards; few could buy them—very few. They used colored paper and crayons, and cut pictures of flowers and other things out of sales catalogs and wallpaper catalogs. I provided them with paper lace doilies and they made some really cute valentines. I bought a lot of the supplies myself; otherwise they wouldn't have had them. We had good fun with the valentines; the kids always enjoyed that.

We also put on a Christmas program. We didn't have electricity in those days, of course, and depended on kerosene lamps for lighting. This was one of the things we had to contend with. We'd present a couple of simple plays, and sing "Silent Night," "O Come All Ye Faithful," and other traditional songs. Children gave recitations learned by memory. For the little ones, a Santa Claus gave out treats. These were all accepted things in those days. We also had a Christmas tree that the kids enjoyed putting up about a week or so before. They made paper chains for the tree, and brought some decorations from home. We placed candles on the boughs, but didn't light them due to the fire hazard. Always, the tree was pretty, and the kids drew names for the Christmas present exchange. The teacher, of course, received lots of good stuff. It was fun.

On extremely cold mornings, I'd go in earlier to get the fire started. When the kids arrived, they'd hang their wet coats on hooks on the wall by the stove and put their boots around the heater's base. Snow stood quite deep at times, but I always walked to school.

One time we had a scare when one of the kids came down with smallpox. Everyone had to be vaccinated. The district didn't have a nurse, so we went to a doctor to get the immunizations.

At the end of each school year, a picnic was held up the Naneum at Ida Nason's place. The Nasons were a well respected Indian family living in this locality. There was a creek nearby, and everyone brought food for a big lunch. They held a surprise shower for me here in the year I got married. We never thought about nature walks at the picnic in those days. The students were farm kids and already had lots of nature all around them.

I remember a funny incident one time when walking home from school with some of the kids. Sometimes, students stayed to help clean up after classes—sweeping, dusting, and whatever needed to be done. I'd walk home with the kids from the Paul and Barrett families. At the intersection of the Naneum and Watson roads, they'd go east and I went west to the home where I was boarding.

One particular autumn day as we approached the road intersection, we spotted two trees with ripe peaches in the Watson place orchard. One of the boys asked, "Oh, Miss Boedcher, do you suppose we could get a couple of peaches?"

I didn't hesitate at all, saying, "Oh that would be nice!"

In no time at all the boys hopped over the fence. They'd just got started when a man suddenly shouted, "What the ___ do you think you're doing? Get outta there."

That loud voice would've scared anyone! The boys turned and cleared the fence without even touching it. We all ran...teacher too. I swear that voice scared the heck out of me.

Afterward, I found out that it was Mr. Watson (who, as things later turned out, would've been my father-in-law if he'd lived longer). I never did meet Mr. Watson because he died of a heart attack that next summer before my second year of teaching. I've been so sorry since. After I met his son, Ed Watson, my eventual husband, I was told that the father and son were a great deal alike. The day I told Ed about this incident he laughed himself sick, and certainly let everybody know about it.

Another time when walking home, I came upon a baler stalled up by the Watson place. In the fall, balers were taken around from farm to farm to bale up cut hay. As I walked up, I saw someone working underneath. After I passed by, pretty soon I heard this somebody crawling out from under and a voice saying, "Howdy schoolmarm!"

I don't remember what I did, but I know I was so surprised! Here was this great big tall guy coming out from under the baler. Ed Watson later told me it was love at first sight. I don't know, but anyway it was quite a deal.

Mrs. Watson, 2001.

Basket socials were very popular in those days and held in Farm Bureau offices, granges, and meeting halls. Baskets and boxes were decorated—often a shoe box covered with crepe paper and lace. Mostly there'd be fried chicken because everyone expected it, and sandwiches, potato salad, and maybe fruit salad, plus deviled eggs, either pie or cake, cookies, and oranges and apples when in season. After auctioning off the baskets and boxes, you'd sit with your partner and eat right there, with everybody talking and laughing. I suspect the teacher's box sold for more than usual. Teachers were popular, especially the single ones.

I had an especially active social life because I got to know the Christensens well when I boarded at their home. I'd join in at the family get-togethers. I got along very well with their two girls, Edith and Alice, and we'd go to the dances at Fairview. I've known them all my life; our kids even grew up together.

11

Lumber Camp Schoolmarm

ETHEL ROBINSON SAXBY, 1926–27

I was in the third grade when we moved to Ellensburg from Bozeman, Montana. My mother suffered from the cold weather in the Gallatin Valley so we decided to come to Washington. First, we had intended to go to California, but then, because of the Normal School in Ellensburg, my parents decided the Kittitas Valley would be a good place to live. I had one sister, five years older, and she and I could go to college and train to be teachers. My sister didn't go, but I did.

Oh, college was something. For one thing, few men went to the Normal School and those who did were the most popular guys you could ever imagine. I was quite

Washington State Normal School
School colors—red and black.
School yell— Zip, Boom, Bah
Hoo, Gah, Hah
W.S.N.S.
Rah, Rah, Rah

amused at first because the dormitory girls were terrifically interested in me when they found out my name was Robinson. There was a Frank and John Robinson on the college football team, and they were quite sure I must have some connection with those football stars, which I didn't.

I had some delightful classes under Mr. Stephens; he was a fascinating man. I remember one summer when about 25 Sisters enrolled in one of his

classes. They came from various parts of the state because the Sisters operated the Lourdes Academy in Ellensburg at the time. From what I'd heard about Mr. Stephens, who otherwise could be quite frank, he toned the class down a bit because of the Sisters.

Lourdes Academy.
Ellensburg Public Library

Kamola Hall, ca. 1920.
Ellensburg Public Library

I particularly remember Miss Wilmarth, who was a Physical Education instructor. I didn't enjoy the athletic program too much, however, because I wasn't particularly athletic. I got plenty of exercise each day by just taking the long walk back and forth to the college.

In looking back to those years, I now have to laugh about a dance-drama presentation given in the spring of 1924. All of the women from one of the classes wore Roman gladiator outfits and capered about with shields and spears on the grass triangle in front of Kamola Hall. Cars were set around, with the headlights turned on for floodlighting.

I graduated in 1925, but didn't get a school that year. I'd been ailing a great deal and finally had a mastoid operation. It took me all summer to recuperate, so I didn't have a job when school time rolled around in September. A little later, however, some friends told me that the Cabin Creek lumber camp in western Kittitas County needed a teacher.

In January, a boyfriend drove me up to Easton in a Ford Roadster, the kind with a single bench seat and a retractable top. After I talked with Mr. McGinnis, the clerk of the board, we went up to the school. The road, of course, was closed because of snow up that way in January. So we walked along the railroad tracks. It was only three miles and a fairly nice day, so I enjoyed getting out. When we approached the school, I saw the teacher's cottage—a little, faded-pink, two-room house that hadn't been painted in a long time. The schoolhouse stood next door.

It was interesting; I'd never been inside a country school before. There were windows along one side, desks of various sizes, a long low wood-stove, and a drinking fountain in the cloakroom that had to be filled from an outside faucet. A week or so later, I went back to the school to get things shaped up. Of course, people in the lumber camp community were much interested in seeing the new teacher and they were very kind. The youngsters soon came by; I ended up meeting most of them before the first day of school. The faucet wasn't connected during the winter.

A 1924 photo of Ethel Robinson included in her application to the Cabin Creek School. *Elaine Saxby Baker*

To get water, you had to walk about two blocks away to a ditch diverted from Cabin Creek.

I have a delightful memory of a mother of two of the children. She came out to talk to me as I was coming back with a bucket of water and she gave me a loaf of hot bread. I've never forgotten that. It was a delightful welcoming to the community, and I have many happy memories of that lovely person. She was an aunt by marriage of the man I later married. So "Aunt Margaret" became very dear to me. I was a little bit homesick at the time, living there alone in the teacher's cottage. My mother had died when I was 15, and I'd been living with my father and uncle since my sister had married, so I wasn't afraid to be alone, but it was different.

School was held from 9 to 3:30. The district furnished everything—books, pencils, and paper. This was a surprise to me because when I was a schoolgirl in Ellensburg you always had to buy your own books and supplies. We'd go to Craig's Bookstore in Ellensburg with a long list of textbooks we needed. My mother, of course, would be quite happy when she found the right kind of book in my big sister's old school things.

At Cabin Creek, I had a problem juggling classes around—you had to have work scheduled for one group while you were working with another. Anyway, I managed. My salary was $125 a month and I did my own janitor work. I also chopped wood, built the fire, shoveled snow, and carried water. I always had to think about keeping the wood box filled and to remember to throw a chunk of wood in the stove on time. The older boys, however,

Ethel Robinson (center, back) with all eight grades at the Cabin
Creek School.
Elaine Saxby Baker

were very kind about offering to keep the wood box filled and tossing a chunk of wood in the stove. They always wanted to help with things like this; they got out of doing schoolwork for awhile.

The children all walked to school. It was such a short distance to go, just up the street a ways. They went home at noon, though sometimes as a treat we'd eat lunch at the school. At noon, I'd go over to my little house and get a bit to eat and then go back. They'd anxiously wait to hear the mill whistle blow at noon, because that meant they could run home for lunch. If it so happened that class was still being held after the whistle blew, or if someone had to finish something, were they ever indignant! For the men at the nearby bunkhouse, they were called to dinner by a kitchen helper coming out and rattling a huge triangle.

At noon, the train came from Ellensburg bringing mail, fresh bread, produce, and freight. Mr. Flummerfelt, the storekeeper, would take a pushcart that ran on rails out to meet the train at Hubner. He had to push it uphill to the station, but with a load and sometimes a few kids, it could coast back down to the store.

When any of the children expected relatives coming in on the train at noon, it was a bit hard to keep their attention. I remember one little boy who was so excited! He wanted to stand and watch out the window because his baby brother was coming home that day. The baby had been in the hospital for quite awhile. I'll never forget him saying, "This is a great day for the Eyeman family!" We were all interested in everyone's joys and sorrows in this delightful little community. The parents were mostly young with a large number of small children.

They helped each other a great deal in the classroom. The big brothers and sisters had such a nice attitude toward their younger brothers and sisters. I remember a sixth grade girl who was extremely protective of her fourth grade brother. She was quite indignant with me because I expected too much of him. It was a nice attitude, though, and a lot of it came from the homes.

As a rural school teacher, you're certainly on your own. The school board was most helpful, as was Mrs. Lee, the superintendent, who contacted me regularly. Discipline was much different in those days. Though I didn't insist that the children sit with their hands folded in front and their feet flat on the floor as when I'd attended school, nevertheless I had to keep them very much in line. Sometimes it didn't work so well, but on the whole they were a pretty good bunch. I still have crocheted doilies and things that the children gave me at Christmas time.

One time, a father who was greatly disturbed came to see me because I hadn't been teaching arithmetic for a particular grade. He wanted to know why. Well, I replied, the superintendent had said, "Those books are obsolete. I'm sending you new ones. Don't use the old ones anymore." Oh yes, the parents were very much on their toes as to what needed to be done in school and they were most cooperative.

One of my pupils, Eldon Morrison, kept falling asleep during school. When I said, "Don't you go to bed early enough?" there was much giggling among the students. I finally learned that the family house was small with only two or three rooms, so the children slept on cots in the living room. However, the family had lots of company in the evening because they owned one of the first radios in the lumber camp. Eldon couldn't go to bed on his cot until the guests went home. I remember visiting another family who brought in wash benches and covered them with blankets to accommodate guests listening to the radio. Radio was just becoming popular, but everybody already had phonographs. "The Wreck of the Old 97" was just one of the records that everybody always wound up to listen to when they had company.

Field trips weren't emphasized so much back then. I do remember one day, however, when I took the students down the railroad tracks to see a beaver dam near the Easton road. Frankly, the children knew a great deal more about the outdoors than I did.

Going out into the woods on the "Dinky Engine" to observe the men logging was fun for everyone. A charming old gentleman took us out. He'd been a hunter and a trapper in his earlier days, but now was rather semi-retired, though he worked as a whistle punk. A whistle punk stood close to a steam donkey engine and cables strung to a nearby spar tree. After one of the loggers out in the nearby woods attached a choker cable to a newly cut-down tree, the whistle punk blew the signal, alerting everyone that the steam engine was dragging a log in. This was a rather wasteful way of logging compared to later times, because those huge logs knocked down smaller trees when dragged in by the cables. It required skill, however, to bring in the logs and load them onto the logging railway carts.

Skiing was becoming rather popular then. The community was nestled in the hills and the area received lots of snow. After school, the kids skied down a nearby slope. I owned skis but wasn't very brave

Cabin Creek schoolboys, winter 1926–27.
Elaine Saxby Baker

about using them. The kids always had an awful time with teacher because I was afraid of falling forward when losing my balance. Instead, I'd sit back down on their ski trail, ruining the tracks they'd set in the snow. Being young as I was then, it was quite an experience to participate with the kids in their interests. I did manage, however, to get around Cabin Creek on my skis.

In our training as teachers, it'd been rather impressed upon us to maintain a dignified persona and proper demeanor when living in a community. There were a great many things that you didn't do if you were a teacher because it just wasn't proper. I was just terribly impressed with this fact, but one humorous incident in this regard has stuck in my mind.

After the whistle had blown and school was out, I'd gone over to the mailbox outside the store to pick up a loaf of fresh bread that'd just arrived on the train. The cookhouse bell hadn't rung yet, so many of the men from the new mill were sitting around on the steps, waiting until supper. It was a beautiful spring day, and I, full of dignity and clutching a loaf of fresh bread, walked back toward the porch of my little house. The kids had been playing baseball and left a bat lying on the ground near the porch. I didn't see it. I stepped on the bat and, in full view of everyone, I fell flat on top of that loaf of bread. I quickly scrambled to my feet and ducked into the house. I had slivers in my chin from landing on the porch! It was really funny, though nobody laughed, but my dignity certainly was wrecked for that day.

During the summer between the two sessions that I taught up there, windows were put into the south side of the building, too. It was nicer; more sunlight came into the room. An addition also was built at the end of the building; the floor there was raised up about eight or nine inches. My desk stood there on this little kind of stage. I'd been interested in drama when at college, so I had various short plays in mind that we could put on. We held quite a few school programs. Several of the local young married couples also put on a play that turned out to be a lot of fun. Everyone was most enthusiastic about supporting and attending events at the school. When we put on plays, even men from the bunkhouse came because they'd heard it'd be quite interesting.

There was a provision in the teaching contract that if you got married, then you were out! No married woman could teach there—a widow perhaps, but not a married woman. I married in the summer of 1927 and that was it.

In the Cabin Creek camp, the homes stood close together and you built your own house. My husband, with the help of men from the community, built ours. You could go to the pile of number-two lumber and get whatever was needed. Most people had just a two or three room house. You only had to pay for windows, nails, and roofing paper.

Everyone lived right there in the camp, including the men who worked in the woods as well as those from the mill. There must've been around 30 men living in the bunkhouse, and at least 20 families. The loggers rode out into the woods on a "kiddy-car" that ran on the lumber railway tracks. It consisted of an old truck engine built into a frame on a railroad car. It was open in front and back, with benches for the men to sit on.

We built our house next door to the schoolhouse in a space directly across from the store. The store stayed open after supper hours, and a good number of men gathered there. They'd sit around and talk for a couple of hours in the evening. When the store closed, you'd see their bobbing lanterns going down the paths as the men went home for the night.

Electricity was available only when the mill was running. However, a local resident, John Morrison, set up a Delco electrical system for people staying through the winter and for those wanting more electricity. They could even run washing machines on the system. If you weren't on the Delco, you only had about 30 watt lights, and they'd go off at 10 pm. Either you sent all of your company home and went to bed, or you scurried around and lit kerosene and gas lanterns.

I remember waiting in line to enter the community shower behind the boiler room. You had to carefully mix cold water with the steam-heated water right at the showerhead to keep from getting scalded. It was important to remember to turn on the cold water first, then add the steam-heated water, and, when through, to turn off the steam before the cold water.

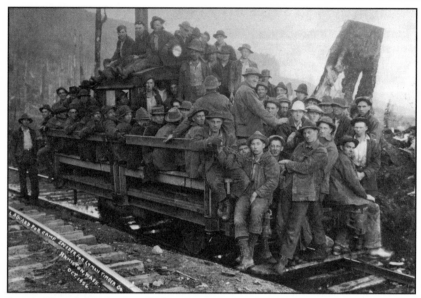

A typical "speeder" in the Cascades logging country.
Ellensburg Public Library

The women were rather competitive—curtains had to be washed regularly, everything scrubbed and scoured, and the children kept just so. Their homes were delightful. I frequently was asked to dinner, and oh, we'd have delicious wild huckleberry and blackberry pies. They were just nice, friendly people. A good many met to play cards in the evening. I'd been introduced to cards a number of years earlier, but just never caught the hang of it. My husband loved to play cards, so I'd go down with him, and sit and crochet or something while the rest of them played card games.

In this friendly community, everyone kind of looked out for each other. When the mill closed at 3 p.m. on Saturday, there'd be quite an exodus of single men and families. Many of the men from the bunkhouse went to Easton for a wild weekend in the "city." People needing a ride, men particularly, gathered at the Cabin Creek store. They'd be ready to go to town and stood around waiting for someone to give them a lift.

When life got too dull at Cabin Creek, Easton was the place to go for night life. Easton had several pool halls and put on dances. Cabin Creek didn't hold dances like at Casland, a large logging camp in the Teanaway area. You had to go to Easton to dance, but I never did.

One time a humorous incident happened to a sawyer named Joe Hastings when he was coming back from Easton in a touring car. He was driving in too fast and hit a bump too hard. The fabric top of the vehicle came down and his head punched right up through it. He drove into camp that way.

A sawyer like Joe Hastings rated rather high in a lumber mill. He was a specialist, as were the high riggers out in the woods who topped and trimmed spar trees and rigged cables. A funny thing I noticed when first coming to the lumber camp was that men had their pant legs cut off about halfway between the ankles and knees. I learned that they needed to have the ankles free and unobstructed when working in the woods. Cutting off the lower pant legs prevented entangling. It was a safety measure.

We knew this nice Norwegian family living down the street. The Petersons were an older couple with a cute little girl who was too young for school at the time I taught. Their little Elsie spoke better English than the parents. One day when driving to town, we offered Mr. Peterson a ride.

I said, "Oh Antone, you look so nice today. I didn't know who you were when all dressed up!"

He replied, "Dis vas de wedden suit. I have it seven year."

When going to town in those days, of course, everyone dressed up.

I liked to occasionally visit my father and sister in Ellensburg, and I didn't have to worry about how my husband would get along when I was away. I merely went over to the cookhouse and asked it it'd be alright if my husband ate there while I was gone. The cook would say, "It's OK. I haven't broken his plate yet," which meant that he was still accepted.

This was a very friendly community and the residents seemed to hold the teacher in high esteem. They were all very nice with me, and I have very happy memories of living there.

Decades later, I returned to the classroom after my dear husband passed away in the summer of 1956. In August, the school at Ronald still didn't have an intermediate teacher. I didn't know many of the people up there, but my husband had worked for Patrick's Coal Company in Ronald for many years and they'd known him. My friend Adeline knew the school board members— she'd had some of them as pupils when she first began teaching years before. Adeline took me to the interview with the school board, and they hired me to teach the third, fourth, and fifth grades. I made mistakes, but I learned as time went on. Sometimes at Ronald, I'd have only the third and fourth grades, and other times the fourth, fifth, and sixth. With three teachers and only about 30 pupils, believe me, the kids received much individual attention.

Then the systems consolidated, and the next year I taught third grade in Cle Elum. I was unhappy there. For the previous 10 years at Ronald, I'd had a lovely room with a view overlooking the mountains. But at Cle Elum, I had an inner room in the building, with mesh bars over the windows and a poor view of the playground.

I taught kindergarten in my last four years and just loved the children. I had 70 pupils the first year, split into morning and afternoon groups. Indeed, I was busy with 35 in each class, but kindergarten I really liked.

12

Is the Ocean as Big as Our Wheat Field

Emma Darter Utz, 1934–60s

Emma Darter Utz, 1990.

I graduated from four years at the Normal School just as they were changing from a two year to a four year curriculum. I went back at different times until I had six years in two majors, English and Education, and minors in art and music. The college office provided places to apply and I got my first job in the fall of 1934.

I started teaching at an isolated school down in Asotin County, in the far southeast corner of Washington. The school stood 30 miles from any sizeable town. It was adjacent to the Blue Mountains on the Oregon side of the Washington-Oregon border, but the state line went right through the farming community. The roads were just one lane dirt tracts. In order to pass when you met somebody on a hillside, one or the other had to go uphill a bit.

It was a seven month school and I earned $60 a month. I paid $16 for board and the woman of the house did my washing. I slept in an upstairs room without heat. Sometimes in winter the temperature fell way below zero in that high country. I walked almost two miles to school, often through knee deep snow. One of the little boys would arrive early at the school and build the fire for me.

It was a one room building. The blackboards consisted of flooring nailed on the wall and painted black. I did have chalk, but used a rag for an eraser. The maps were torn and had holes so I had to draw my own maps. The children's desks were the old fashioned iron and wood type screwed to floor runners, with box-like desks and hinged seats.

I believe I started the day with a bell, and I must've had seven or eight children. There was no lunch program; the youngsters brought their own lunches and water. At recess we played "ante over," throwing a ball over the schoolhouse, and also tag and baseball games. I generally did the pitching. One time, some of the boys who'd already graduated came by and wanted to play too. After one reached third base, he became so excited, jumping up and down, that the next runner went right past him and came in to home plate ahead of him and they both were out.

Another time this little boy, who'd never hit the ball in his whole life, was up to bat. I was pitching and didn't expect him to hit it, so I looked over my shoulder. He hit it alright, and the baseball got me right in the side of the face. He was so upset.

But a teacher didn't dare let them know you're upset. The kids also brought in snakes. "Oh Miss Darter, I have something pretty for you." They couldn't understand it when I didn't cringe or squirm.

I emphasized reading and math, and also geography because I knew they needed help when a youngster asked, "Is the Pacific Ocean as big as our wheat field out there?" I did have the state study guide for each grade and that helped. Our books were whatever they had at home and whatever the superintendent could find. She was only able to provide us with one current textbook for each class. Of course, there was no money during those Great Depression years. Families provided their children with the supplies they needed. This was better, however, than when a school furnished these materials because the kids didn't waste things, break pencils on purpose, or tear up paper. When families had to pay, the kids were more careful.

The people in that isolated rural locality were very nice. We went for hayrides, danced at the grange hall, and held picnics and potlucks. My school also prepared a Christmas program; we were expected to include something of a religious nature, as well as humorous plays and other fun activities. The Christmas program was held at the grange hall along with two other schools, which made for a pretty good show. We had a basket social and that's where I met my future husband; he bought my basket.

One time when practicing for the program, the little brother of my husband-to-be got real silly and wrapped himself up in the stage curtain. I grabbed him by the hair and slung him off the stage. He was a good little boy then. Later, he even came up and asked me to marry his big brother, so I guess discipline was good for him. When I think of some of the things teachers did, they'd fire you for that now.

We didn't go on field trips. Coyotes, cougars, and bears abounded in outback Asotin County, and also when I taught up at Ronald in Kittitas County. The youngsters were scared to go out.

They were such well behaved kids in those days. I hardly had any trouble with discipline. Even the eighth graders were just as charming as they could be. Of course, in those days their folks thrashed them good when they got home if brother or sister told on them.

I remember one discipline problem though. A boy had already graduated from the eighth grade and his folks didn't want to send him to high school, so they shoved him off on me. He was a holy terror. I finally told the parents they had to take him out of school or I was going to report him to the superintendent.

In one of the schools in the locality, the students would lock the teacher in the building, and then go out to play and wouldn't come back. The big boys even gave the teacher a spanking if they felt like it. Finally, a man who'd been a school teacher was asked if he'd take over. Three young women teachers had already quit the school. This fellow said he would, "If you'll let me do it my way."

When he took over the school, students still tore all around the first day or two. They were just as obnoxious as they could be. These were older boys who didn't attend school in the fall, and left early in the spring, to help out on the farm. On the third day, the teacher brought a black snake whip with him. He whipped those kids; really, he would've been convicted for it now. Everyone was disciplined after that!

To get to the Christmas program at the grange hall, people came on horseback or in a wagon or buggy. Everyone used horses because the roads weren't plowed for cars during the winter in that remote section of Asotin County. The county didn't bother with clearing the snow, yet this was one of the oldest rural communities in the area. Sometimes, snow stood two or three feet deep, but we never had to close the school. We went sleigh riding, which was lots of fun; we'd end up at somebody's house and have a taffy pull. It was like the pioneer days.

I married in the spring of 1935, and my husband and I moved to the Kittitas Valley. I taught in a one room school up Manastash Creek to finish out another lady's term. I earned $60 a month. I had to walk quite a distance to school because the people I boarded with lived up the middle fork (that area is closed off now; you can't even get up there). The district knew I was married. Earlier, married women weren't allowed to teach, but apparently that had changed by 1936, or it didn't make any difference in a rural school.

The teaching pattern at Manastash was typical. For recitation exercises, small groups of students came up front and sat on a bench by the stove. When finishing their recitations, they returned to their desks, and then another group came up. All the while, of course, I also had to keep the children who were sitting at their desks doing something useful.

I next taught the upper grades at the Damman School just southwest of Ellensburg. I received $108 per month. Damman had two teachers for grades one through six. I taught the fourth, fifth, and sixth grades. The other teacher and I took turns fixing the hot lunches, and we did our own janitorial work. I probably taught nine or ten children, and then the next year switched to the primary grades. I taught here for two years. We had more supplies at the Damman School because there was more money.

One time, a youngster came to school with the measles and it wasn't long until all the other youngsters were out sick. When the first boy came back to class after being home for awhile, he was the only one to arrive. Needless to say, we didn't stay all day.

Around this time, my husband and I started a family and I had to be at home. Eventually, I substituted all around the Kittitas Valley for a decade or so. In a few years—after my children were in school and big enough to be left alone a little while in the afternoons—I taught one year at the Woldale School, also in the Ellensburg vicinity. That was a thing I liked about teaching; I could arrive home soon after my children did.

Next, when the county superintendent said, "There's a vacancy at Ronald if you want it," I thought it sounded interesting. The drive up to Ronald in the wintertime, though, could be *very* interesting! I taught the first three grades, Ethel Saxby the next three grades, and a male teacher had the seventh

Woldale School, District #13, ca. 1929–30.
Ellensburg Public Library

and eighth graders. The school had four rooms altogether, one of which was used for handicapped children from all over the county.

One time the board came for a surprise inspection. Luckily, I'd washed the blackboards the night before and had put up my assignments very neatly when the board members came walking in, sat down in back, and never said a word. The youngsters were just precious; they studied so hard and remained so quiet. After the board left, everybody sighed with relief. I think the students were afraid that their folks might find something out. As one little girl said, "Oh, if we're not good in school, we always have a brother or a sister who will tell on us, and then we get spanked at home with the polenta stick."

Polenta was a cornmeal mush, particularly popular with the foreign born workers. It was stirred with a big stick and that's what the parents used to give a spanking. My kids that day didn't want to get spanked when going home, and they were good. I always let them laugh when something was funny, and I let them cry, too. Everybody cried together if someone got hurt.

A few people on the school boards could be difficult. I think some of them had very little education themselves and here was a chance for them to somehow make up for it with overbearing intentions. At one school, a board member made things so unpleasant that I quit. He wouldn't allow us to buy a new flag because, at this time in the late 1950s, Alaska and Hawaii were about to gain statehood and the American flag would be adding two stars. He didn't want to waste money on a new flag. So in the afternoon, I'd stay after school mending the school's old weather beaten flag. He also drew a line around the piano to be sure I didn't move it.

Ronald was a close knit community. When a PTA meeting was held, grandmas, uncles, aunts, and just everybody came and made a party of it. Oh, they were nice people and lots of fun. If they needed something from Ellensburg and didn't have time to make the trip, they'd ask me to bring it up. Then they'd give me homemade raviolis, which were so good.

They weren't mining at that time; most of the men were working in the timber industry. Each morning when driving to work, I'd meet one particular log truck when going around a big curve by the Presbyterian Church. One time—fortunately I was five minutes late—the chains holding the logs had broken and the truck lost its load on that curve. The driver thought for sure he'd dumped them on me.

One day, the reading consultant suggested we drive to Easton and see what their school facilities were like. We went up that afternoon. Mr. Carlson showed us around the building, and when returning to his office, he offered me a job. This sounded so much better, though it was a further drive, but

I'd be on the main highway in case anything happened. I taught there for 12 years. These were two and three teacher schools, with several grades in a room. You were your own boss, and I worked there until I retired.

On one occasion, I took the children out to a ranch where the owner showed them corn on the stalk, and beans and cucumbers on the vines. The youngsters living up there in the cooler climate of western Kittitas County had never seen garden stuff growing. It was interesting to them.

I made a little over $3,000 a year at Easton, and our household could afford to buy a new car for my commute. A new car sold for under $4,000 and gas was cheap, so it didn't cost much to drive. A good house went for $4,500. The good times of the 1950s were a far cry from the Depression years, when I first started teaching in Asotin County.

13

The Seats Went Ka-Bang

May Spurling Jankowski, 1939–42

I graduated from Ellensburg High School in 1935. I'd always wanted to be a Home Economics teacher since I'd been in 4H. A that time, though, the Normal School didn't have a program for graduating Home Economics teachers, so I went into General Education. I took the four year course. In Washington in those days, however, you could teach with a three-year diploma. Since there was a surplus of teachers and not a lot of jobs, and because I was close to finishing a four-year degree and college didn't cost much back then, I kept right on going.

Many of us went to college due to the lack of jobs during the Depression and because it was quite inexpensive. Fees were low, and I rode an Ellensburg school bus to the college. We didn't need to buy books; we used the library. Textbooks were on reserve and could be taken home at night for our assignments and brought back next morning. Students needed to buy very few books during four years of college.

Mrs. Michaelsen in a Home Economics class had us keep a record of expenses. It cost me only $200 during my fourth year. By living at home, riding a school bus, not buying books, and with non-existent lab fees, college costs were reasonable.

I didn't get a lifetime certificate because by the time I started teaching they no longer were given out. In 1938, in fact, the campus was filled with older teachers trying to get credits in the last year that lifetime teaching certificates were available. When I graduated in 1939, we would be required to return to college every six years to pick up so many credits.

I remember Mr. Beck who taught science classes and how to teach reading. Miss Hebeler taught penmanship. We also had to do our student teaching; it was accomplished in two quarters at different times rather than in a whole block. I first did sixth grade at the Washington School, and the following year went back there to do the third grade. I also took one quarter at the campus school at the intermediate level. We took instruction in both primary and intermediate. You had to go to one of the bigger colleges in those days to teach in high school. The Normal School wasn't authorized to graduate high school instructors.

I was much involved in off-campus activities. Quite a few of the girls had to earn their living while going to college and stayed at homes in the nearby community, aiding the families. So, the off-campus group—including a lot of us who were locals—was quite an active bunch. We held parties and did a lot of things together. At that time, of course, there probably were four women to every man at the college.

We went to roller skating parties, treasure hunts, and so on, and in those days attended formal dances in Nicholson Gym. It was kind of hard to find a man to dance with, but we wore our long dresses and took part anyway. Football was played out at the fairgrounds, and basketball at the gymnasium, coached by Mr. Barto. In fact, a number of the buildings on campus came to be named for professors who taught there when I attended: Barto, Hertz, Hogue, Hebeler, Smyser, and Shaw.

The school where I taught, Upper Naneum, was pretty much what I expected. As a youngster I'd attended Woldale—a two room school having primary (first though fourth grade) and intermediate (fifth through eighth). Most of the schools in the valley were one room buildings. I was familiar with most of them; Dad loved to drive around and we'd seen practically every one in the area. The Upper Naneum School was nicely painted white and had a

May Spurling's students at the Upper Naneum School: (l. to r.) Joanne Nason, Lillian Bunger, Larry Gleason, John Nason Jr., Lemoyne Henderson, Janice Cleveland, and Richard Carlson.
May Spurling Jankowski

neat old barn and two outhouses. Everybody around there had outhouses, which was par for the course in that area—no sewer lines, not many septic tanks, and no electricity.

There was a stage in the building, and a woodshed and cloakroom. A hand pump and sink in the cloakroom allowed the students to wash their hands in cold water. The school's big round wood stove had a protective cover around it to prevent people from getting burned. It was flat on top and we kept a teakettle or pan there so we'd have some warm water. At that time, the government gave out food supplies and the school districts received them—flour, cereal, some fruit and beans, and so on. Parents prepared and brought the hot lunches to us. In cold weather, the parents took turns. We had all kinds of goodies, and the parents were good cooks.

The desks were screwed on floor-board runners. To move the desks, you had to slide whole sections of them. They were the old fashioned wood and iron type with flat desk tops. The desk top opened up to allow students to store their books and supplies. The hinged seats went "Ka-Bang!" when put up.

We did very well for supplies in a district that wasn't particularly wealthy. I got curtain cloth to make curtains for the tall windows. I had all the chalk I needed and the children were provided with books, though they brought their own pencils, tablets, and crayons. We had a small library, and I'm sure, some dictionaries.

I walked 1½ miles to school from Mrs. Charlton's, where I boarded. I maintained the fire throughout most of the year. In the winter, one of the Minor boys came up from their ranch just below the school and started the fire early. Even when spring came, it could be quite cold, and I needed to get the stove going.

Sometimes I rode a horse to school, but I don't recall that any of the students did. I think Mr. Bunger, who lived at the end of a canal intake, brought his daughter Lillian down, but everybody else walked. They all lived within walking distance of the school—the Nasons, an Indian family, resided a mile or so up the road, the Carl-

Ida Nason.
Ellensburg Public Library

sons lived over a hill to the east, and the Hendersons down the road a ways, about as far south as the end of our district.

After the first bell rang and the students arrived, it was an honor for a child to pull the bell again, indicating the time to go in and take their seats. We probably did the flag salute and sang a song or two. That was what rural schools did.

Upper Naneum kids, 1940.
May Spurling Jankowski

I usually started with the first grade. Many of the children in those days were oriented to working on their own. If they had a math assignment due the next day, then they did that while the first graders recited. I next went to the second grade; I just had four grades that first year. We followed the book pretty closely—going to page so and so. They didn't need a lot of direction to get busy and were good about not interrupting while I worked with a class. They didn't come around asking lots of questions and were very independent workers.

I can't remember particularly if they helped each other, but I suppose they could've if needed. Usually we had reading and math. I don't think I ever wrote down a schedule. But I indicated on the board, or displayed somewhere, who did what and when. They were so quiet. That's the thing I noticed in those bigger rooms; the children were so quiet. Out in the country like that they tended to be very respectful.

Rural teachers taught it all, including music. One of my former teachers from the Woldale District gave me lots of musical ideas. I marched the kids around, played musical games, sang nursery rhymes, and all those types of things. The older students needed to focus more time on social studies. Art projects included drawing pictures of the seasons and making their own holiday cards for Valentine's Day, Christmas, Mother's Day, and Halloween. Valentine's Day, of course, was very popular. Each student had a box for the other kids to put valentines in.

Ray Green, the county superintendent, came out a couple of times. When the state mandated hearing tests, he brought out an audiometer. I tested all the children for their hearing.

Christmas programs were a big deal in rural schools and required a lot of practice. Everything had to be just right—the songs, a little play, and, during my first year, a nativity scene. Racial perceptions could be an issue in those days, but having the little Indian girl, Joanne Nason, playing Mother Mary was no problem at all. In that community, the John and Ida Nason family were well accepted. Some of the people there might've thought a darker complexioned girl being Mother Mary was unusual, but they perfectly accepted it.

Clara Charlton, who was on the school board, had been a teacher and gave me a lot of her material for the Christmas play. The program was held at night with gas lanterns providing the lighting. (We also had used gas lanterns at my parents' home on Reecer Creek out of Ellensburg; that area didn't get electricity until 1938.) I talked my brother into being Santa Claus. He came dressed as Santa Claus and passed out treats and gifts to the students. When my brother began to leave, the grandchildren of the lady I was boarding with ran out after him, wanting to see Santa's sleigh. He had a hard time getting away.

For the second year's Christmas program, Ralph Charlton's daughter was Santa Claus. The third year it was Mrs. Lillian Dunning. She lived up Wilson Creek north of Ellensburg and had been Santa Claus at Woldale when I was in school. I talked her into coming over. She hadn't forgotten how to be Santa Claus and was so good. My Santa suit got used quite a bit over the years.

The other big event was the end-of-year picnic. Rural school policy required this and all the families came. The Nasons, residing a mile or so up Naneum Creek, owned a nice area for a picnic, with big trees, a lot of quaking aspen, and some little bushes along the creek. For seating, we had

Upper Naneum School picnic on the John Nason property.
May Spurling Jankowski

folding chairs, mainly from the school, and boards set on sawhorses. We held races, ballgames, and things like that. We were lucky those years; the weather was good. There'd probably be 25 to 30 people. Dads in those days were pretty much available, since they farmed and could take an afternoon off. All the fathers were farmers, except Mr. Bunger, who was a city water control employee on Naneum Creek. Ellensburg had water rights up there.

Fairview off to the southeast had a big hall for dances and other events. We didn't hold dances at the Upper Naneum School. Nor did we have box socials. I do remember them at Woldale way back when I was in school, but not in the time period I'm talking about. I also didn't have to worry about any state or county tests. After school activities were never held because by the time classes let out at 4 p.m., it usually was starting to get dark. Besides, most of the students had chores to do at home—especially the older kids in the fourth, fifth, and sixth grades.

The Nasons, an Indian family, fit in very well and were just part of the community. Ida Nason was quite eager to have her children do things right and do what the teacher said. In fact, all the parents in that particular area were encouraging and wanted their children to do the best they could. That's what school's all about!

Appendix A

Eighth Grade Examination, 1913

* * *

Office of Superintendent of Public Instruction, Olympia[1]

My Dear Superintendent and Teachers:

Herewith are sent lists of questions to be used by pupils of the Eighth Grade who are candidates for certificates of graduation. The aim of these questions is to give the pupils of the Eighth Grade a test in both the technical and general knowledge which they should posses in order to be ready for the higher work. The following facts have been kept in view in the preparation of the questions: 1. The advancement of the pupils. 2. The general knowledge that they should possess. 3. The supplementary work that is now expected of teachers in our schools. 4. The requirements of the preparatory courses in higher schools.

If a pupil succeeds in passing successfully this test, he will receive a certificate of promotion, and will be entitled to enter upon a high school course.

Permit the suggestion that no teacher have charge of his pupils while they are writing upon the questions, and to this end the superintendent or someone appointed by him should have charge of the room during examination.

The papers are to be graded by the Eighth Grade examiners by law. The standard is uniform for the state, and is as follows:

Minimum .... 60 per cent
Minimum in grammar and arithmetic .... 80 per cent
Average .... 80 per cent

The rules and regulations for teachers' examinations are to be followed so far as they are applicable.

Yours truly,
Mrs. Josephine Preston,
Superintendent of Public Instruction

* * *

Eighth Grade Examination Questions
May 15 and 16, 1913
Program of Examination

Thursday

A.M.	P.M.
Grammar	History and Civics
Spelling	Geography

Friday

A.M.	P.M.
Arithmetic	Physiology
Reading	Reading Circle Work

The General Questions may be answered at any convenient time.

GENERAL QUESTIONS
[Note. - Examiners will grade penmanship of pupils
from their answers to the following questions.]

1. Write your name in full.
2. What is your age?
3. Write your post office address, number of your school district, and name of your teacher.
4. To what grade of the school do you belong? Have you completed the grade?
5. Is this your first eighth grade examination?
6. If you succeed in obtaining an eighth grade diploma, do you expect to attend school next term? Where?

ARITHMETIC[2]
(Answer ten only.)

Mental—
1. (a) A man spent three-fifths of his money and had $60 left, how much had he at first?
   (b) Find the cost of 348 pounds of veal at 25¢ a pound.

Mental—
2. (a) What is the cost of 1215 yards of flannel at 33 1-3¢ a yard?

(b) Berries bought at 8¢ per quart are sold at 12¢. What was the per cent of gain?

3. Make out a bill supplying place, date, name, and amount of bill.
   Grapes, 53 baskets, 20¢ per basket.
   Plums, 6½ bu., 20¢ per peck.
   Cherries, 4 bu., 12¢ per quart.
   Pear, 2 bu., 30¢ per peck.
   Pie Plant, 20 bundles, 5¢ per bundle.

4. Simplify the following:
$$\frac{(2\text{-}3 + 4½) \times (3\ 1\text{-}3 - 1½)}{2½ \times 3\ 1\text{-}3}$$

5. Mr. Ames owns a 50 foot lot fronting on a street 60 feet wide from curb to curb. He is assessed 1-3 the cost of paving. Find the cost of the paving to him at $2.93 per sq. yd.

6. A farmer bought 75 acres of land at $50 an acre paying 1-3 cash and giving his note for the balance due in 3 yrs. 6 mos. with interest at 6%. What was the amount of this note at maturity?

7. Find the amount of taxes paid on 80 acres of land valued at $20 an acre, assessed at four-fifths of its value, if the rate of taxation is 21 mills for general tax and 52 mills for school tax.

8. Write the following numbers and find their sum: eight hundred and eighteen thousandths, six hundred twenty-five ten thousandths, sixty and two tenths, nine hundred five hundred thousandths, three hundred ten, seven and six hundredths.

9. What is the meaning of the following terms: fraction, integer, denominator, quotient, multiplicand.

10. (a) Extract the sq. root of 1814.76.
    (b) If the diameter of a circle is 12 ft. what is the circumference?

11. How many acres in a field 180 rods long and 56 rods wide? How many rods of fence will it take to fence the field in two lots each 56x90 rods?

12. Find the cost of the following:
    30 dozen eggs at 24¢ a dozen.
    25 pounds and 4 ounces of butter at 32¢ a lb.
    1560 pounds of potatoes at $16 a ton.
    15 tons, 5 cwt. of hay at $13½ a ton.

GEOGRAPHY
(Answer ten only.)

1. Name five states located in different parts of the U.S. and give a leading industry in each.
2. Name and locate two countries that are engaged in war in Europe at the present time.
3. Name at least four ways that the Mississippi river affects the life of citizens of the United States.
4. How do you account for the fact that Labrador is termed "Frozen Labrador" while France which is in nearly the same latitude, is known as "Sunny France?"
5. Prepare a suitable bill of fare for a dinner containing five different articles of food from different countries and tell where each was raised.
6. Why is a winter day shorter in this state than a summer day?
7. Sketch a map of the state showing four large cities, three chief mountains and three of the largest rivers.
8. Explain briefly why each of the following has become a large city: Chicago, Minneapolis, New York. St. Louis, Berlin.
9. What are the characteristics of a good harbor? Name at least four cities having excellent harbors.
10. Name and define four land formations.
11. Give a good reason why each of the following named places would be of interest to a visitor to that place: (a) Egypt; (b) Central America; (c) Paris; (d) Kimberly; (e) Rome.

GRAMMAR
(Answer ten only.)

1. The teacher will dictate the following sentences at the beginning of the examination period: (1) John, come here. (2) Did you hear me, John? (3) On the sixth day of January, 1813, the inhabitants of a lonely dwelling

near a certain city in Germany, were in great alarm. (4) May I go too? There will be two others.

(Examiners will grade on spelling, capitalization and punctuation.)

2. Give five rules for the use of capital letters, and illustrate each.
3. Use the plurals of the following nouns in sentences: Valley, beau, mystery, fish, life.
4. Write one of the following business letters:
   (a) To a business man asking for work on Saturdays.
   (b) To a firm ordering books or other goods.
5. Use the noun "man" in sentences in two different constructions in the objective case. Use the noun "brother-in-law" in a sentence in the possessive plural.
6. Define and give examples in sentences of three kinds of complements.
7. Give the use of the infinitives in the following sentences:
   (a) He went to see the show.
   (b) He is hard to please.
   (c) It is a sin to tell lies.
   (d) Nothing remains but to g...[3]
8. Diagram or analyze: It was...a matter of curiosity who the old gentleman w...
9. State four common errors in English. Show the correct form of each in sentences.
10. Write a sentence containing a verb in the plural number. Write five irregular verbs and give the principal parts of each.
11. Write one of the following notes:
    (a) To a friend explaining why you cannot keep an appointment.
    (b) To your teacher explaining an absence.

HISTORY AND CIVICS
(Answer ten only.)

1. Write a short account of the Iroquois.
2. Tell of the work of the Cabots.
3. Why is each of the three of the following to be remembered: Yeardley? Bradford? Calvert? Stuyvesant? La Salle?
4. Give one cause and one result of the French and Indian War.
5. Explain the nature and purpose of the Townshend Acts.
6. What effect had each of the following events on the course of the Revolutionary War: (a) Battle of Lexington? (b) Surrender of Cornwallis?

7. Name the vice-president of the U.S. By whom and for how long was he elected?
8. Explain each of the following: (a) Emancipation Proclamation (b) Kansas-Nebraska Bill.
9. Make a short statement concerning the work of two of the following: Grant, Clay, Dewey.
10. Give three powers of and two prohibitions on Congress.
11. When and under what circumstances was one of the following acquired by the United States: (a) Philippine Islands? (b) Porto Rico?
12. Name two political parties which took part in the presidential campaign of 1912. Who was the candidate for each party?

PHYSIOLOGY AND HYGIENE

1. Name and locate ten bones in the human body.
2. How may bacteria in food be destroyed?
3. Why is sleep necessary to good health? State several rules regarding sleep.
4. State several rules which, if followed, would stamp out tuberculosis.
5. State several things which would improve the sanitary conditions of most school rooms.
6. Of what use is saliva in digestion?
7. Name the organs of digestion.
8. Describe the heart and its functions. How may it be kept in best condition?
9. What are the main ways in which deafness occurs?
10. What diseases are spread through the schools? How may they be reduced?

READING
(Answer ten only.)

1-5. Have each pupil read one selection in prose and one in poetry from the grade reading book.
(These selections are to be designated for this county.)
6. What do you consider is good oral reading?
7. Name one selection each from five American poets.
8. Give a quotation from a favorite selection in your textbook. Why do you like this particular selection?
9. Name a humorous selection. A patriotic poem. A historical poem.

10. Who wrote the following:
    (a) The Great Stone Face.
    (b) The King of the Golden River.
    (c) The Golden Touch.
    (d) The Legend of Sleepy Hollow.
    (e) Hiawatha.
11. Write a brief review of a selection in your reader including the principal characters, the scene and leading events. Make this not more than three-quarters of a page.
12. Who wrote the "Star Spangled Banner?" What circumstances called forth the writing?

READING CIRCLE WORK

Write a brief review of one reading circle book.

SPELLING

(The examiner will explain or define any word which may be spelled in more than one way.)

1. falsely	51. complement
2. embarrass	52. business
3. breathe	53. camera
4. council	54. carrying
5. borne	55. color
6. coupon	56. fossilize
7. caramel	57. lodgment
8. census	58. malaria
9. nectar	59. library
10. neigh	60. lose
11. noisily	61. mileage
12. noble	62. lodger
13. iris	63. compliment
14. government	64. mortgage
15. juvenile	65. muscle
16. emerge	66. notably
17. merrily	67. desert
18. poultice	68. lilac

19. hymn
20. breath
21. libel
22. tenement
23. unloosen
24. valuing
25. auxiliary
26. gorilla
27. bridal
28. dissatisfy
29. heir
30. iciness
31. cylinder
32. celery
33. bridle
34. chords
35. misspell
36. pennant
37. roguish
38. salad
39. rein
40. nay
41. surety
42. absent
43. altar
44. affect
45. character
46. grammar
47. hideous
48. bankruptcy
49. barricade
50. blaspheme

69. lavish
70. lacing
71. launch
72. idealize
73. sheriff
74. new
75. principal
76. reptile
77. poplar
78. recommend
79. valleys
80. yolk
81. tinge
82. tepid
83. principle
84. knew
85. trestle
86. alter
87. cords
88. pedler [*actual spelling on list*]
89. issuing
90. parallel
91. capitol
92. shoulder
93. reign
94. vanilla
95. weasel
96. tragedy
97. sorrel
98. surge
99. tariff
100. wholly

* * *

1. This 1913 Eighth Grade Examination is archived at the Washington State Historical Society, EPH-B 979.704 W276e 1913. It is presented here unabridged with only slight modification in layout, primarily being the alphabetical rearrangement of subjects.
2. On this particular document, the following answers in Arithmetic were penciled in: 1. (a) "150," 1. (b) "$87," 2. (a) "$405," and 2. (b) "50%."
3. This portion of the original document has a tear and hole.

Appendix B

State of Washington Teachers' Examinations, 1914

This exam was not meant to be taken in its entirety at one time, as evidenced by two different topics been tested during most of the time slots (e.g., GERMAN or PHYSIOLOGY at 8:00 A.M., BOOKKEEPING or ORTHOGRAPHY at 9:30 A.M., etc.). Topics were assigned specifically and in groupings to satisfy whichever teacher qualifications were needed for a variety of certificate requirements and diplomas. The tests vary in achievement levels, and some appear to be elective choices, such as German, Latin, Bookkeeping, and Music. This document is preserved at the Washington State Archives, Central Regional Branch. It is presented here unabridged with only a slight modification in layout.

* * *

STATE OF WASHINGTON
Uniform Questions
for
Teachers' Examinations
May 14, 15 and 16, 1914
Prepared by the State Board of Education

Questions for Thursday

GERMAN.
(Thursday, 8:00 A.M.)

1 and 2.

(a) In elner Schule waren zwei Knaben, Hans and Fritz, die von ihren Eltern sehr schlecht irzegen wurde und daher eine Freude darin fanden uberall Schaden anzurichten und nutzliche Dinge zu verderben.

In der Schule schnitten sie heimlich allerlei Figuren in die Bänke und Fritz schnitt sich einmal den Finger ab. Gingen sie abends auf der Strasse, so schlugen sie mit grossen Stocken an die Fenster oder zogen an den Klingeln der Häuser und liefen dana schnell fort und versteckten sich. Em Mann aber Hess Ihnen mehrere Abende aufpassen und endlich gelang es ihm sie auf der Tat zu ergreifen. Er uberlleferte sie der Obrigkelt und sie wurden zum Gespotte ihrer Mitschuler.

(b) Explain: darin, in die Bänke, abends, liess ihnen, aufpassen, gelang es ihm, schnitt sich, den Finger ab.

3. Name the class of nouns and state how the plural of each is formed.
4. (a) When are vowels regularly long? (b) When are vowels regularly short? (c) Give at least two rules for each.
5. Give principal parts, third person singular present tense, and the imperative second person singular of the following verbs: geben, bitten, beten, leiden filegen, schliessen, raten, anfangen, aufstehen.
6. (a) Give the synopsis of *sehen* in the passive voice.
   (b) What are substitutes for the passive in German?
7. (a) Decline in singular and plural: my large book, the great forest, this beautiful flower.
   (b) Translate: Such a pen, such a man, all her money, a little money, something good, nothing else.
8. (a) Give the German modals and the meanings of each.
   (b) What two ways may English *will* be translated?
   (c) What peculiarity have the modals when they govern a dependent infinitive?
9. (a) Translate, changing into indirect discourse: Karl said, "I will come tomorrow."
   (b) Translate: He said that they had gone.
   (c) Give rule for indirect discourse.
10. Translate:
    (a) To whom shall I give this book?
    (b) Marie could have written her exercises if she had wanted to.
    (c) Without threatening him, I commanded the servant to stand up, so that I might see what he had put in his pocket.
    (d) You are probably right, but I would not like to go so far.
    (e) The children to whom we had explained these mistakes were not pupils of this school.

PHYSIOLOGY.
(Thursday, 8:00 A.M.)

1. Describe the structure of the process of decay in teeth.
2. Explain how the heat of the body is maintained and regulated.
3. What bodily activities are under the control of the sympathetic nervous system?
4. Trace the changes starch foods undergo before being used by the tissues.
5. Name the different substances of which the blood is composed and state the functions of each.
6. What are the disadvantages of a purely vegetable diet?
7. By what means are the germs of infectious diseases transmitted from one person to another?
8. Describe the process of food absorption.
9. Describe the mechanism for a reflex action. Use illustration.
10. What first aids should be rendered in case of a serious burn, a cut artery, a broken arm?

BOOKKEEPING.
(Thursday, 9:30 A.M.)

1. Define Bookkeeping. What two methods are in general use?
2. Define Debit and Credit.
3. What is meant by books of original entry? Name three.
4. What is a trial balance? Does it prove the accuracy of all of your work? Tell why.
5. Define Notes Receivable; Notes Payable.
6. Explain how to find the loss or gain in any resource account having an inventory.
7. What is meant by the term "At five days sight?"
8. Can the credit side of the Cash Account exceed the debit side? Tell why.
9. What is the purpose of a Purchase Ledger? Sales Ledger?
10. W.B. Haeseler paid F.H. Arnold in full of account his 15 days sight draft on H.J. Oke for $250; H.J. Oke honored the draft by accepting same. Draw up a form of the day book Journal and show the necessary entry for each of the three parties to this transaction.

ORTHOGRAPHY.
(Thursday, 9:30 A.M.)

1 to 5, inclusive.

1. registration	26. disappoint
2. separate	27. chauffeur
3. promissory	28. tragedy
4. hygiene	29. definite
5. complement	30. prejudice
6. extraordinary	31. disease
7. derogatory	32. receipt
8. memorable	33. simultaneous
9. vaccination	34. genitive
10. hypotenuse	35. prairie
11. participle	36. embarrass
12. euphony	37. apparatus
13. automobile	38. eligible
14. impregnable	39. Cincinnati
15. laboratory	40. cemetery
10. finally	41. tariff
17. occasion	42. coincide
18. similarly	43. criticise
19. description	44. omitted
20. homologous	45. weird
21. immediately	46. quotient
22. accommodate	47. absence
23. coefficient	48. Caesar
24. balance	49. allotment
25. appearance	50. exaggerate

6. Mark diacritically: turtle, gimlet, vacuum, ask, apparatus, heinous, mediaeval, ecclesiastic, conciliation, drama.
7. Give a rule for the correct use of ie and ei in spelling. Give three exceptions to the rule.
8. Define and illustrate: homonym; synonym; syllable; suffix; primitive word.
9. What advantages, if any, are secured by having the child prepare his spelling lesson on the day before he is to recite it?
10. How may the child be taught to make the words which he has learned in the spelling lesson a part of his every day vocabulary?

GEOGRAPHY.
(Thursday, 10:30 A.M.)

1. (a) Mention three important wheat producing regions of the world outside of North America.
   (b) Where is the world's best market for wheat?
2. Mention ten articles which your grocer probably gets from foreign countries and tell from what country each article may come.
3. (a) How are sponges obtained? In what place are they found most abundantly? (b) How are pearls obtained? In what place are they found most abundantly?
4. Mention three kerosene oil producing regions of the world. Two diamond producing areas.
5. How are the customs and habits of mankind affected by (a) topography; (b) climatic conditions; (c) character of the soil; (d) occurrence of valuable minerals?
6. Name the five largest cities in the United States, and the five largest in Europe.
7. What is the leading industry in each of the following: (1) South Africa; (2) Kentucky; (3) Alaska; (4) Massachusetts; (5) Argentine Republic?
8. Where is the Suez Canal? Why was it built, and what nation controls it?
9. What is the chief occupation of the people of New England? Why do they follow this particular line of industry?
10. What cargo would a ship be likely to carry from Philadelphia to Liverpool? From Manchester to Bombay?

GRAMMAR.
(Thursday, 1:00 P.M.)

1. Explain the meaning of the following terms and illustrate by citing an example: irregular verb, antecedent, clause, adjective phrase, object complement, retained object, defective verb, inflection.
2. Give the plural form of the following nouns: cod, alms, basis, focus, apparatus, series, spoonful, looker-on, knight-templar, brother.
3. Give three rules for forming the plural of compound nouns, and give examples illustrating each rule.
4. Give the principal parts of the following verbs: hit, see, eat, go, give, forget, sink, be, lie, set.

5. Parse the italicized words and expressions in the following sentences:
   (a) She has left me *lonely*.
   (b) They paid *me* the money.
   (c) I choose *to go*.
   (d) I believed him *to be honest*.
   (e) He was often taken *to be I*.
6. What do you do when you parse an adjective? Write a sentence and illustrate.
7. Analyze: "When I said I would die a bachelor I did not think I should live till I were married."
8-9. Write a letter to a superintendent of school applying for a teaching position.
10. Ten credits will be assigned this paper on the basis of neatness, form and style.

LATIN.
(Thursday, 1:00 P.M.)

1. Translate:
   Haec cum pluribus verbis flens a Caesare peteret Caesar elus dextram prendit; consolatus rogat, finem orandi faciat; tanti eius apud se gratiam ease ostendit uti et rei publicae iniuriam et suum dolorem eius voluntate ac precibus condonet.
2. Explain the use of each subjunctive verb in the above passage.
3. Explain the construction of orandi, tanti, voluntate.
4. Make a diagram or table illustrating the rule for sequence of tenses.
5. Name five uses of the subjunctive in dependent clauses.
6. Translate into Latin and explain the grammatical construction illustrated in the following folk sentences
   (a) The Helvetians learned that Orgetorix had sent many ambassadors to Dumnorix.
   (b) They did not know whether Caesar would receive them in surrender or not.
7. Translate:
   His de rebus Caesar cortior factus et infirmitatum Gallorum veritus, quod sunt in consillis capiendis mobiles et novis plerumque rebus student, nihil his committendum existimavit.
8. Explain the construction of the italicized words in Question 7.

9. Give a synopsis of the verb "rego" in the third person singular; active and passive.

10. Translate and explain the grammatical construction illustrated in the following sentences.

   (a) The Germans, having conquered Gaul, were not able to enter within the territory of the Belgians.

   (b) This must be done by the Sequanians.

PENMANSHIP AND PUNCTUATION.
(Thursday, 3:00 P.M.)

Write correctly:

The young man it is often said has genius enough if he would only study now the truth is as i shall take the liberty to state it that genius will study it is that in the mind which does study that is the very nature of it i care not to say that it will always use books all study is not reading any more than all reading is study

By study I mean but let one of the noblest geniuses and hardest students of any age define it for me study says Cicero is the persistent and intense occupation of mind directed with a strong effort of will to any subject such as philosophy poetry geometry letters such study such intense mental action and nothing else is genius

GEOLOGY.
(Thursday, 3:00 P.M.)

1. Discuss the work of the three dominant geologic processes as shown in continent making, mountain building, mountain sculpturing, and erosion of valleys.

2. What agencies are most effective in the formation of residual soil, transported soil, sedimentary rock? Describe their work in each case.

3. Define erosion and describe the relations of the processes included under the general term. Under what conditions is wind an important erosive agent? Describe its work.

4. Discuss the work of ground water in the metamorphism of rocks, in the solidification of sediments, in formation of metallic veins, in production of surface features.
5. How would you distinguish between young and old valleys, young and old mountains, young and old shore lines?
6. What conditions favor the formation of glaciers? How do they move? Describe typical features produced by glacial erosion.
7. What is the cause for and evidence of changes of level in land masses? How do these changes produce earthquakes? What is the effect of submergence or depression on an ocean shore line?
8. Explain the use of fossils and rock formations in determining former geographic and climatic relations on the earth's surface.
9. Under what conditions were coal beds made and preserved? In what geological periods were valuable coal deposits formed in America? Name localities for each period.
10. Discuss evolution of the earth and present conditions of interior (a) according to the Nebular Hypothesis, (b) according to the Planetesimal Hypothesis.

Questions for Friday

ARITHMETIC.
(Friday, 8:00 A.M.)

1. (a) What proportion of arithmetic should be oral?
(b) Why is it desirable to have a portion of the problems required of pupils indicated rather than solved? (That is, having the processes necessary for solution shown without working out the problems.)
2. Should pupils be encouraged to estimate results before solving a problem? Give reason.
3. A rectangular field that contains 40 acres is four times as long as it is wide. Find its dimensions.
4. A man bought two horses for $360, paying 25% more for one than for the other; he sold the cheaper one at 12¼% loss and the dearer one at 30% gain. What was the net gain and the rate of gain?
5. At 33 1-3% ad valorem the duty on woollen goods invoiced at $1.25 per yard, was $800. How many yards were imported?

6. Find the amount of $1,572 borrowed Jan. 16, 1907, and repaid May 4, 1908, at 6%.
7. Originate a problem to fit the following statement: 4X5X6 divided by 2X6 =Cost.
8. What things do you need to know in order to
   1. Compute the area of a rectangular field?
   2. Compute the perimeter of the above field?
   3. Compute the area of a triangle?
   4. Compute the number of loads of earth to be removed from an excavation for the foundation of a building?
   5. Compute the number of tons of coal which a bin will hold?

9. Which gives the lower price for a piano listed at $600, a direct discount of 45%, or successive discounts of 25%, 15% and 5%? How much lower?
10. How many yards of 27-in. carpet are required for a room 15 ft. wide and 24 ft. long, not allowing for waste in matching?

GEOMETRY.
(Friday, 8:00 A.M.)

1. Distinguish between axiom, postulate, proposition and corollary.
2. State three cases in which triangles are equal. Prove one of them.
3. How is the side of an oblique triangle opposite an acute angle expressed in terms of the other side? State and prove the above theorem.
4. The altitudes of a triangle meet in a point. Prove.
5. Given an oblique triangle, A, B, C. Draw a line through the triangle parallel to one side, dividing the triangle into two equivalent parts. Prove.
6. A straight line moves so that its ends constantly touch two fixed rods which are perpendicular each other. Find the locus of its middle point.
7. Find the relation between the side of a regular hexagon and the side of a regular triangle inscribed in the same circle.
8. The bisector of an angle of a triangle divides opposite side into segments which are proportional to the adjacent sides.
9. Find the radii of the concentric circles that divide a circle 12 inches in diameter into three equivalent parts.
10. The radius of a circle is 10 inches. From a point 20 inches from the center a secant is drawn so that the internal segment is 5 inches; find the length of the segment.

CIVICS.
(Friday, 10:30 A.M.)

1. Through what three stages has territorial government usually passed?
2. Why was a federal judiciary deemed necessary? Give an outline of its organization.
3. What are the duties of a prosecuting attorney?
4. When is a city of the first class, second class, third class, fourth class?
5. How is a councilman recalled?
6. What is a writ of Habeas Corpus? When refused? What has it been called? How issued? Its origin?
7. Give six qualifications of a juror.
8. Who are exempt from acting on jury?
9. What aliens may be admitted as citizens of the United States?
10. When is it necessary to have a congressman at large and how is he elected?

POLITICAL ECONOMY.
(Friday 10:30 A.M.)

1-2. Give the history of the making of a pen knife or a pair of shoes, and use correctly in the description the terms *extractive industry, production, capitalist, interest, wages, profits, rent, labor.*
3. Why is it that men desire to get control of coal, gas, oil, and water power?
4. Was it economically wasteful for the early pioneers to cut down and burn trees in order to get land to plow? Would it be wasteful to burn timber in the same way today? What makes the difference?
5. Explain the relation of an oversupply of middle men in trade to the "high cost of living."
6. What is the law of diminishing returns? Illustrate it by the improvement of a piece of land.
7. France produces more wheat to the acre than the United States. Does this prove the inefficiency of American farming methods? Would a greater expenditure of labor and capital per acre have been a wiser agricultural policy on the part of the American farmer 50 years ago?
8. Has the cheapening of products by improved methods of production affected the real wages of labor?

9. How do laws which protect women workers or regulate hours affect the level of competition? Why is this desirable?
10. What is the effect of a rising standard of living upon the increase of population? Compare this with Malthus' law of population.

THEORY AND ART OF TEACHING.
(Friday, 10:30 P.M.)

1. How far may instruction in morals be carried into the public schools?
2. As a means of mental training, what are the specific ends to be kept in view in teaching arithmetic?
3. What place do reviews hold in teaching and how may they best be handled?
4. Discuss the professional obligations of the teacher. Include in this a reference to the Teacher's Retirement Fund.
5. How is emulation an incentive to study?
6. Name five points to be considered under the hygiene of the school.
7. (a) Aside from improving general appearance, of what value are good pictures on the walls of the school room?
   (b) List ten well known pictures suitable for school room decoration.
8. To what extent should pupils be allowed to work together? What are the principles governing the allowing of pupils to work together?
9-10. Discuss the chapter on "Memory" from Sabin's Common Sense Didactics.

HISTORY.
(Friday, 1:00 P.M.)

1. Under what conditions was local self-government established in Virginia?
2. When and for what reasons did the English acquire New York?
3. Mention three causes of Bacon's rebellion.
4. Why was the battle of Trenton important?
5. Explain the nature of the government under the Articles of Confederation.
6. What was each of the following: Whiskey Rebellion? Jay's Treaty? Sedition Law?

7. Outline briefly the campaigns of the War of 1812.

8. What were the results of the war with Mexico?

9. What was the Kansas-Nebraska bill? State the effect of this bill in party development.

10. What amendments were made to the Constitution as a result of the Civil War? To what extent are their provisions recognized?

GENERAL HISTORY.
(Friday, 1:00 P.M.)

1. Who was Homer? Solon? Zeus? Pisistratus?

2. Explain the connection between the Confederation of Delos and the Athenian Empire.

3. Mention two reasons why Alexander of Macedon should be called "The Great."

4. How many wars were there between Rome and Carthage? Give the results of the wars.

5. Summarize the work of Charlemagne.

6. What were the Crusades? Mention the leaders and two results of the Crusades.

7. What was the nature and purpose of each of the following: Inquisition? Society of Jesus?

8. Explain each of the following terms in connection with the religious movement in France: Huguenots, St. Bartholomew's Day, Edict of Nantes, Rochelle.

9. State briefly the religious policy of the two Stuarts, Charles II and James II.

10. In connection with the Napoleonic Era explain the following: Tilsit, Code Napoleon, Trafalgar, Confederation of the Rhine.

ZOOLOGY.
(Friday, 2:30 P.M.)

1. Define: (a) zoology, (b) protozoa, (a) metazoa, (d) bug, (a) brachiopod.

2. In what respects do birds resemble reptiles?

3. Name the sciences treating of the following groups of animals: (a) insects, (b) fishes, (c) birds, (d) fossils, (e) shells.

4. Compare the blood circulation (heart) of: (a) man, (b) frog, (c) fish, (d) clam.
5. Classify the following: (a) oyster, (b) earth worm, (a) snake, (d) bat, (e) whale.
6. What can you say about the habits and reproduction of aphis?
7. What resemblances are there in the structure of corals and jellyfishes?
8. Distinguish (a) between homology and analogy; and (b) show why the former is used as a basis for classification.
9. Give three representatives of the arachnida.
10. Write the classes of vertebrates in order from lower to higher.

STATE MANUAL.
(Friday, 2:30 P.M.)

1. Give a brief account of the explorations of Geo. Vancouver in the Northwest.
2. When did Washington become a territory? When a state?
3. Enumerate five powers and duties of county superintendents.
4. What are the provisions of the law regarding contagious diseases, malignant and non-malignant?
5. What is the minimum length of a school day for primary grades? For higher grades?
6. What is the penalty for failure to keep the school register according to law?
7. Enumerate three powers and duties of the county board of education.
8. State the different kinds of common school certificates provided for by law which are to be issued by the State Superintendent of Public Instruction. What certificates are county superintendents empowered to issue?
9. Who have the power to revoke certificates?
10. State the law regarding the age of applicants for certificates.

MUSIC.
(Friday, 3:30 P.M.)

1. (a) Name five composers and a composition of each.
   (b) Name a noted vocalist, pianist, violinist, orchestra director, and band master.

2. Of what significance are the following terms: allegro, a tempo, andante, crescendo and staccato.
3. Write the sign of treble and bass staffs.
4. Name six kinds of rests. Illustrate six kinds of notes.
5. What training in music have you had?
6. What is the use of the dot, tie, slur, sharp, and flat?
7-8. Give five reasons why music should be taught in a systematic manner in the public school.
9. Write the signatures of A flat, B flat, C, B, and D.
10. (a) Name the tones of the scale.
    (b) Write the scale of G indicating steps.

Appendix C

Rules for Teachers and Pupils, 1918

* * *

Rules and Regulations Adopted by the
(Washington) State Board of Education[1]

Teachers.

1. The teachers in the public schools of this state shall follow the prescribed course of study and enforce the rules and regulations of the State Board of Education; shall keep records, use blanks and render reports according to instructions.

2. Teachers shall be held responsible for the care of all school property entrusted to them; shall frequently inspect the same and promptly report to the district clerk any damage it may have received.

3. Each teacher shall prepare a program of daily exercises, a copy of which shall be posted in a conspicuous place in the school room.

4. Teachers shall exercise watchful care over the conduct and habits of the pupils while under their jurisdiction.

5. Teachers shall maintain strict order and discipline in their schools at all times. Any neglect of this requirement shall be considered good cause for dismissal. Corporal punishment may be resorted to when it becomes necessary to the preservation of proper discipline. No cruel or unusual punishment shall be inflicted; and no teacher shall administer punishment on or about the head of any pupil.

6. In any case of misconduct or insubordination, when the teacher deems it necessary for the good of the school, he may suspend a pupil, and shall immediately notify the directors of the district thereof for further action, and shall send a copy of said notice to the parents or guardians of the child.

7. Every public school teacher shall give vigilant attention to the temperature and ventilation of the school room and shall see that the atmosphere of the room is frequently changed.

8. Teachers shall have the right, and it shall be their duty, to direct and control within reasonable limits the studies of their pupils: *Provided*, That all pupils shall receive instruction in the branches included in the prescribed course of study.

9. The use of tobacco in any form or place by a teacher is discountenanced, and the use of alcoholic stimulants in any form or place as a beverage is prohibited. The use of tobacco or any other narcotic on the school premises by a teacher shall work a forfeiture of his certificate.

10. The teacher shall make an estimate of the worth of each pupil's work in the several subjects as often as once every two months. This estimate should be based upon the pupil's daily work, together with such tests as the teacher may deem it advisable to give during the period.

    At the close of every term of school the teacher shall thoroughly examine, in all necessary branches, all pupils whose work has not been satisfactory and shall leave in the school register a statement of the work completed by each pupil in each subject. He shall also leave a record of the deportment of each pupil.

11. Teachers shall require excuses from the parents or guardians of pupils, either in person or by written note, in all cases of absence, tardiness or dismissal before the close of school, and no excuse shall be deemed valid except that of sickness. Excuses for absence shall be placed in the hands of the attendance officer, and it shall be the duty of said attendance officer to investigate thoroughly each case and enforce the provisions of the law relating thereto.

12. An attendance of less than one hour at any half day's session shall not be counted by the teacher in making his or her annual report.

13. Teachers are enjoined to encourage exercises in composition and declamation, including memorization of choice selections and quotations. In the preparation of programs for rhetoricals, teachers shall use every effort to secure selections of a high literary character.

14. Teachers are required to be at their respective schoolrooms at least thirty minutes before the time of opening school in the morning and fifteen minutes before the opening of school in the afternoon.

15. Teachers are required to make due preparation daily for their duties, such preparation to include attendance upon teachers' meetings and other professional work contributing to efficient school service, which may be required by the superintendent, principal, or board of directors.

Pupils.

1. Every pupil shall be punctual and regular in attendance, obedient to all rules of the school, diligent in study, respectful and obedient to teachers and kind and obliging to schoolmates.

2. Willful disobedience, habitual truancy, vulgarity or profanity, the use of tobacco, stealing, the carrying of deadly weapons, the carrying or using of dangerous playthings, shall constitute good cause for suspension or expulsion from school.

3. As soon as dismissed, pupils shall leave the school premises and go directly to their homes. Loitering on the way to and from school is positively forbidden.

4. Pupils shall give attention to personal neatness and cleanliness, and any who fail in this respect may be sent home to be prepared properly for school.

5. Pupils shall not be detained more than forty minutes after the regular hour for dismissal.

* * *

1. *From the first page of the 1918 Damman School attendance register, in the Ellensburg Public Library archives.*

Appendix D

When were figures first used for arithmetic in Europe?

How long does it take light—which travels 192,-000 miles per second—to come from the sun?

What gems symbolize the months July, August and September.

Describe the Sphinx, sculptured from the rock, near the Pyramids at Gizeh, Egypt.

Give some statistics about the Great Pyramid of Gizeh, Egypt.—the most extensive structure ever erected by man.

In what country of Europe do the peasants light their cigarettes by means of pocket flint and steel?

If a man could jump as far in proportion to his height, as a flea, how far could he jump?

Who was known as the "knight without fear and without reproach?"

What are the famous Roman catacombs?

Why do we say of an active worker "He worked like a Trojan"?

Give the history of the Obelisk known as Cleopatra's Needle, in Central Park, New York City.

Where may a boy or girl get free information about industrial schools, or about how to earn a living?

What colors have been adopted for mourning, historically, in various countries?

What is the most interesting bell, historically, in America?

What planet is our nearest neighbor?

3

Sample pages from *The Electrical Wonder Book* (Salem, Massachusetts: Parker Brothers, 1910). In this educational game, a player spins the pointer to randomly select one of the questions in the circles. The correct answer for each question is included among the circles on the opposite page. The game encouraged reading and gaining knowledge.
Little Schoolhouse Collection, Kittitas County Fairgrounds

8 minutes, 13 seconds; to come from the nearest fixed star, light requires over three years—from Sirius, 22 years.

Figures were introduced into Europe by Saracens from Arabia, 991. Before that year, letters were used.

The carnelian,—cure of evils resulting from forgetfulness; onyx,—conjugal felicity; chrysolite,—preservation from folly.

107 1-2 feet long, 53 feet high. Only its human head visible; desert sands conceal the lion-like body.

488 feet high; covers over four acres; begun 2170 B. C.; cost $145,000,000. 5,000,000 tons of hewn stones employed.

In European Turkey. Many peasants, also, use sickles to cut their grain.

If Washington Monument were placed on top of the Singer building, he could jump over them both.

Chevalier Bayard (1475-1524), a famous French captain, who was so brave and generous as to win this title.

Tombs about three miles from Rome, consisting of long underground passages where bodies of early Christians were picked.

The reference is to the heroic labors of the Trojans to save their city, Troy, from the Greeks.

Set up in Egypt, 1831 B. C. Moved to Alexandria by Augustus Caesar. Presented to U. S. 1880.

Write to the National League for Industrial Education, Newark, N. J.; or New York City; Springfield, Mass., Chicago, and other offices.

In Europe and America, black; in Turkey, violet; China, white; Egypt, yellow; Ethiopia, brown; Salvation Army, white.

Mars, which most nearly resembles the earth, and is probably inhabited.

"Liberty Bell," cast in London 1752 for Penn. State House. Recast in Philadelphia, 1753. Rung at Declaration of Independence.

Bibliography

Kittitas Valley History

Brown, Joseph C., ed. *Valley of the Strong: Stories of Yakima and Central Washington History*. Yakima: Westcoast, 1974.

Centennial Committee of Central Washington University. *Central Remembered: A Collection of Memories and Anecdotes*. Ellensburg: CWU Auxiliary Services, 1992.

Dow, Edson. *Passes to the North: History of Wenatchee Mountains*. Wenatchee Bindery, 1963.

Ellensburg Daily Record. "Ellensburg City Light: Powering the Community for 100 Years, 1891–1991," June 17, 1991 [16 page special newspaper insert].

_____. *Kittitas County Historic Photo Album*. Portland: Pediment, 1999.

_____. *Kittitas County Memories*. Portland: Pediment, 2003.

Ellensburg Public Schools. "Kittitas Valley Pioneers." 1995 [For third grade use].

Ficken, Robert E. *Washington Territory*. Pullman: Washington State University Press, 2002.

Glauert, Earl T., and Merle H. Kunz, eds. *Kittitas Frontiersmen*. Ellensburg Public Library, 1976.

Grandstaff, Hilton. "Memories of Cabin Creek: The Community and the Mill, 1925–1940." Typescript w/photos, 1993, Ellensburg Public Library, NWREF/634.98/Grandstaff, H.

Henderson, Eugene M. *The Pine Tree Express*. Author copyright, 1990.

(An) Illustrated History of Klickitat, Yakima and Kittitas Counties with an Outline of the Early History of the State of Washington. Interstate, 1904.

Kittitas County Centennial Committee. *A History of Kittitas County, Washington, 1989*. Dallas: Taylor, 1989.

Lewty, Peter J. *Across the Columbia Plain: Railroad Expansion in the Interior Northwest, 1885–1893*. Pullman: Washington State University Press, 1995.

Mohler, Samuel R. "Boom Days in Ellensburg, 1888–1891." *Pacific Northwest Quarterly*, Vol. 36, No. 4 (October 24, 1945).

_____. *The First Seventy-Five Years: A History of Central Washington State College, 1891–1966*. Ellensburg: Central Washington State College, 1967.

Prater, Yvonne. *Snoqualmie Pass: From Indian Trail to Interstate*. Seattle: The Mountaineers, 1981.

Renz, Louis T. *The Construction of the Northern Pacific Railroad*. Author copyright, 1973.

Smith, Leta May. *The End of the Trail*. Hicksville, New York: Exposition Press, 1976.

Splawn, A.J. *Ka-mi-akin: The Last Hero of the Yakimas*. Caldwell, Idaho: Caxton Press, 1917.

Superintendent of Public Instruction. *Biannual Reports*, Vols. 1909–1910, 1919–1920, 1922–1923, 1927–1928. Olympia: Washington Public Documents.

Undergraduate/Graduate Catalogs. Central Washington University Archives, RG 007-04-07, Registrar Services: Box 1 - 1892–1915, Box 2 - 1916–1940.

Wing, Robert C., ed., et al. *A Century of Service: The Puget Power Story*. Bellevue: Puget Sound Power and Light Company, 1987.

Children's Books

Brooks, Edward. *The New Normal Mental Arithmetic: A Thorough and Complete Course by Analysis and Induction*. Philadelphia: Sower, Potts, 1873.

Chase, Annie. *Stories of Industry*. Boston, et al.: Educational Publishing, 1913.
[Upper elementary extra reading]

Clark, J. Erskine. *Chatterbox*. Boston: Dana Estes, 1878–1933.
[An American large-format annual reprint of numerous articles and items from an English weekly children's magazine; *Ellensburg Public Library*.]

The Electrical Wonder Book. Salem, Massachusetts: Parker Brothers, 1910.
[*Little Schoolhouse Collection, Kittitas County Fairgrounds*]

Elson, William Harris. *The Elson Readers: Pre-Primer through Book Eight*. Chicago: Scott, Foresman, 1909–27.
[Sight word method. The pre-primer in the series, the "Pupil's Hand Chart," is a small book version of wall charts presented by a teacher; *Donna Nylander*.]

Fish, Herbert Clay. *Our State of Washington*. New York, Chicago: C. Scribner's Sons, 1927.
[Upper elementary extra reading; *CWU Special Collections*.]

Gates, Arthur I. *Peter and Peggy: The Work-Play Books Series, Primer*. New York: Macmillan, 1930.
[Reader with sight word method; *Kittitas Valley Museum*.]

Horn, Ernest. *Horn-Ashbaugh Speller: For Grades One to Eight*. Philadelphia: J.B. Lippincott, c1926.
[Teacher guide; *CWU Special Collections*.]

Ocker, William August. *Physical Education for Primary Schools: Informal Gymnastics in Lesson Form with Piano Accompaniment*. New York: A.S. Barnes, 1926.
[Teacher guide; *CWU Special Collections* and *Kittitas Valley Museum*.]

Peter Coddle's Trip to New York and What He Saw There: A Comical Combination of Curious Circumstances for 100 Evenings. Cincinnati: Peter G. Thomson, 1882.

Potter, Milton Chase. *Oral and Written English: Book One–Two*. Boston, New York: Ginn, 1917.

Price, Overton W. *The Land We Live: The Book of Conservation*. Boston: Small, Maynard, c1911, 1917.
[Upper elementary extra reading; *CWU Special Collections*.]

Sheridan, Bernard Matthew. *Speaking and Writing English: Fourth Grade*. Chicago, New York: B.H. Sanborn, 1924.

Smith, Roswell Chamberlain. *Smith's First Book in Geography: An Introductory Geography Designed for Children*, 8th Edition. Portland, Maine: Sanborne and Carter, 1848.

Spaulding, Frank Ellsworth. *Aldine Readers, Book One*. New York: Newson, 1918.
[Sight word method]

Starch, Daniel. *The Test and Study Speller*. Boston, New York: Silver, Burdett, 1921.
[Teacher guide]

Washington (State) Superintendent of Public Instruction. *English: A Course of Study for Use in the Elementary and Secondary Schools of Washington*. Olympia: F.M. Lamborn, 1921.
[Teacher guide]

Schoolbooks in the Little Schoolhouse Collection, Kittitas County Fairgrounds, Ellensburg

Arithmetic

Wentworth and Reed. *Wentworth's Primary Arithmetic*. Boston: Ginn, 1890.
[Each child with a copy read along with the teacher. Mostly story problems with some drill; begins with counting, proceeds to fractions and percentages.]
Level: 1st to 4th grades.
Donor: Robert Lange (1988), son of Phare Lange, teacher at Wilson Creek School, District #1, Kittitas County, 1913.

Stone and Mills. *The Stone-Mills Arithmetic: Primary*. Boston, New York, Chicago: Benj. H. Sanborn, 1914.
[Begins with counting, continues to multiplication and division; half drill, half story problems.]
Level: 1st to 4th grades.
Donor: anonymous.

_____. *New Stone-Mills Arithmetic: Advanced*. Boston, New York, Chicago: Benj. H. Sanborn, 1911, 1914, 1920.
[Emphasis on practicality in the business world and accounting; story problems and some algebra/geometry.]
Level: 7th to 8th grades.
Donors: Ronnie Lee (book used by Floyd Lee, brother of Freda Olds).

Stone, J. *The Stone Arithmetic: Advanced*. Chicago, New York, Boston: Benj. H. Sanborn, 1925, 1927.
[Focus on business, insurance, banking, stocks; emphasis on algebra, geometry, theoretical.]
Level: 7th to 8th grades.
Donor: Wendell Prater family (1993).

English

Brautigan, Harper, and Kidd. *The Progressive Composition Lessons: Book One, Third and Fourth Years*. Boston, New York, Chicago: Silver, Burdett, 1912.
[Copy is heavily poured-over and marked. Stories end with composition questions—oral exercises, oral composition, written composition, spelling, correction exercise. One of the first stories is "Little Red Riding Hood."]
Level: 3rd to 4th grades.
Donor: anonymous.

Beveridge, Ryan, and Lewis. *English for Use: Book Three*. Philadelphia: John C. Winston, 1926.
[Color plate frontispiece; focus on sentence parts, grammar, verb tenses, rules, and exercises. A written assignment (1931) by a student, "Pauline," remains folded inside the book; printed in ink with a nibbed pen, with teacher's corrections in faded red at the top.]
Level: 7th to 8th grades.
Donor: Wendell Prater family (1993).

Geography

Carpenter, F. *Carpenter's Geographical Reader: South America*. New York, Cincinnati, Chicago: American Book, 1899.
[A well worn 6" x 8" volume. Includes colored maps, b/w photos (unusual for this era), and written as a travelogue using the pronoun "we," which includes the reader in the journeys. Touches all aspects of travel in addition to the destinations—personal travel needs, ocean currents, passports, etc. Lively engaging style; informal, entertaining, and informative.]
Level: 5th to 8th grades.
Donor: anonymous.

Atwood, W. *New Geography: Book Two*. Boston, et al.: Ginn, 1920.
[Front cover is missing. A 9½" x 11½" format, with photos and colored maps; very dry presentation.]
Level: 6th to 8th grades.
Donor: anonymous.

McMurry and Parkins. *Elementary Geography*. Macmillan, 1921, 1928.
[A 10" x 18" format in conversational style, with colored maps, colored prints, and b/w photos. Relates information in a child's life.]
Level: 6th to 8th grades.
Donor: anonymous.

Wheeler and Holmes. *Burton Holmes Travel Stories: A Series of Informational Silent Readers, Japan, Korea and Formosa*. Chicago: Wheeler, 1924.
[A 5½" x 8" format, with informal supplementary material and b/w photos. Semi-conversational in style.]
Level: upper elementary.
Donor: anonymous.

Rolf, M. *Our National Parks: Book Two*. Chicago, New York, Boston: Benj. H. Sanborn, 1929.
[A 6" x 8" format, with color plate frontispiece and b/w photos. Includes conversations between two families in cars traveling across the United States visiting National Parks.]
Level: upper elementary.
Donor: anonymous.

Nida and Webb. *Our Country Past and Present: A Unified Course in the History and the Geography of the United States for Elementary Schools*. Chicago, Atlanta, New York: Scott, Foresman, 1930.
[An 8" x 10" format, with color frontispiece and colored maps. Has a narrative style; follows textbook trend of combining geography and history.]
Level: upper elementary.
Donor: anonymous.

Stull and Hatch. *Journeys Through Many Lands: A Textbook in the New Geography, Our World Today*. Boston, et al.: Allyn and Bacon, 1934.
[An 8" x 10" travelogue narrative. About half of the pages are filled with color maps and b/w photos.]
Level: upper elementary.
Donor: "For our precious 'Gerald Hunt School' from its first superintendent, Christine Bettas, a retired Ellensburg teacher" (1987). A second copy also was given by an anonymous donor.

_____. *Our World Today: Europe and Europe Overseas*. Boston, et al.: Allyn and Bacon, 1934, 1935, 1938.
[An 8" x 10" format, with a dry informative style, but includes photos, graphs, or maps on nearly all pages.]
Level: 6th grade.
Donor: anonymous.

Johnson, O. *A Picture Book of Children around the World*. Cleveland: Harter, 1934.
[A 9" x 12" paperback, with large photos of children in ethnic dress and full captions.]
Level: elementary.
Donor: "Clara Charlton" inscribed in book.

History

[Title page missing] *Barnes Elementary History of the United States*. New York, Cincinnati, Chicago: American Book, 1902[?].
[Well worn and falling apart; narrative style, with numerous b/w pictures.]
Level: elementary.
Donor: "Maude Gardinier" inscribed in book.

Mace, Dietzler, and Fink. *A School History of the United States*. Chicago, New York, London: Rand, McNally, 1904.
[Still stiff as if seldom used, with 10 color plates, b/w drawings. A rather dry style of presentation.]
Level: 6th to 8th grades.
Donor: "Alice Gardinier" inscribed in book.

Thwaites, Kendall, and Paxton. *A History of the United States for Grammer Schools*. Houghton-Mifflin, 1924.
[Well worn and falling apart; an engaging story-telling style.]
Level: 7th to 8th grades.
Donor: Ray and Evelyn Razey (1980).

Vannest and Smith. *Socialized History of the United States*. New York, et al.: Charles Scribner's Sons, 1931.
[Color plates and b/w pictures. Sectioned into topics, with titles such as "How the United States Is Peopled," "How Our Home Life Has Changed since Colonial Times," etc. Perhaps more interesting than a strict "chronology of events" approach.]
Level: 7th to 8th grades.
Donor: anonymous.

Music

Smith, E. *The Common School Book of Vocal Music: The Modern Music Series*. New York, Chicago, Boston: Silver, Burdett, 1904.
[Meant for ungraded classrooms, specifically the one room school so common at the time. Older students learned the music and taught it to the younger students. Music was a subject in which mixed grade children could participate together.]
Level: elementary.
Donor: anonymous.

McLaughlin and Gilchrist. *The New Educational Music Course: Second Reader*. Boston, et al.: Ginn, 1904.
[Songs, notation, rhythms, two part singing.]
Level: 5th grade.
Donor: anonymous.

Linden, A. *Songs for Common Schools*. Chicago, Philadelphia, Des Moines: Laurel, 1914.
[Well worn and falling apart; a teacher's piano book of popular and patriotic songs.]
Level: elementary.
Donor: Ralph Lynch estate (1983).

Physiology and Hygiene

Krohn, W. *Graded Lessons in Hygiene: Pupil's Edition*. Olympia, Seattle, Tacoma: Westland Park, 1900.
[Well used; dark lined illustrations appear to be engravings. Conversational style about food, drink, body function, and maintaining health.]
Level: intermediate grades.
Donor: Louis Brain (brought in by Eleanor Brain).

Haviland, M. *Modern Physiology Hygiene and Health: The Most Wonderful House in the World, the Mechanics and Hygiene of the Body*. Philadelphia, London, Chicago: J.B. Lippincott, 1921.
[Well used; b/w illustrations. Health facts presented in appealing story form, with rules to follow after each section.]
Level: 3rd to 6th grades.
Donors: Evelyn and Ray Razey.

_____. *Modern Physiology Hygiene and Health: Good Neighbors, a Study in Vocational and Community Hygiene*. Philadelphia, London, Chicago: J.B. Lippincott, 1922.
[Stresses good health for being a good worker and earning a better income. Skeleton, muscles, and body parts named and illustrated with b/w drawings; prepared students for the eighth grade exams.]
Level: 7th to 8th grades.
Donors: Evelyn and Ray Razey.

Reading

Baldwin, J. *Baldwin's Readers: School Reading by Grades, Fourth Year*. New York, Cincinnati, Chicago: American Book, 1897.
[Stresses distinct enunciation as important, and inculcates appreciation for literature, patriotism, and morality. Includes a few b/w drawings.]
Level: 4th grade.
Donor: anonymous.

_____. *Baldwin's Readers: School Reading by Grades, Sixth Year*. New York, Cincinnati, Chicago: American Book, 1897.
[Offerings from famous writers and patriots. Assumes sixth graders to be skilled, insightful, and critical readers.]
Level: 6th grade.
Donor: anonymous.

_____. *The Fairy Reader: Adapted from Grimm and Anderson, Eclectic Readings*. New York, et al.: American Book, 1905.
[Large print. Much loved book, falling apart with first 22 pages missing.]
Level: 1st to 3rd grades.
Donor: anonymous.

Grover, E. *The Art-Literature Series: A Primer*. Atkinson Mentzer, 1904.
[Early example of change to shorter texts, with emphasis on a child's interests.]
Level: primer.

Gordon, E. *The Gordon Readers: First Book*. Boston, New York, Chicago: D.C. Heath, 1902, 1910, 1912.
[Well used. Phonics, rhyming, controlled vocabulary, and uses some McGuffey methods.]
Level: 1st grade.
Donor: anonymous.

Fassett, J. *The Beacon Second Reader*. Boston, et al.: Ginn, 1914.
[Sight word method. Old stories, folk legends, and fairy tales of literary merit rewritten for the second grade level.]
Level: 2nd grade.
Donor: "Myrna Prater" inscribed in book.

Edson and Laing. *The Edson-Laing Readers: Book Four, Working Together*. Chicago, New York, Boston: Benj. H. Sanborn, 1913, 1917.
[Emphasis on social-industrial ideas]
Level: 3rd to 4th grades.
Donor: anonymous.

Lewis, Roland, and Richardson. *The Silent Readers: Fifth Reader*. Philadelphia, et al.: John C. Winston, 1920.
[Supplement to oral reading practice]
Level: 5th grade.
Donors: Ray and Evelyn Razey.

Elson, W. *The Elson Readers: Book Three*. Chicago, Atlanta, New York: Scott, Foresman, 1920.
Level: 3rd grade.
Donor: "Louisa Gardinier, Cove School, 1923" inscribed on inside cover.

Dressel, Robbins, and Graff. *The New Barnes Readers: The Kearney Plan, Book Three*. Chicago, New York: Laidlaw Brothers, 1924.
Level: 3rd grade.
Donor: Christine Bettas.

Fassett, J. *The New Beacon Primer*. Boston, et al.: Ginn, 1921.
[First 24 pages missing. Limited phonetic approach, mostly sight words; difficult, with few pictures.]
Level: 1st grade.
Donor: anonymous.

Smedley and Olsen. *The Smedley and Olsen New First Reader*. Hall and McCreary, 1928.
[Includes color illustrations]
Level: various in series.

Rader, Free, and Treadwell. *Storyland: Book Five*. Evanston, Illinois: Row, Peterson, 1930.
[Many hero stories]
Level: 5th grade.
Donor: "Alice Gardinier" inscribed in book.

Stone and Stone. *Webster Readers: Tom, Jip and Jane*. Webster, 1932.
[Extensive color illustrations]
Level: various in series.

Smith, N. *Tom's Trip: Unit Activity Reading Series*. Silver Burdett, 1935.
[40 page paperback pre-primer, with color picture on each page with large-type words. Publishers by this time were breaking up primers into short books.]
Level: 1st grade.
Donor: anonymous.

O'Donnell and Carey. *Rides and Slides: The Alice and Jerry Books*. Row, Peterson, 1936.
[48 page paperback pre-primer, with color picture on each page with large-type words.]
Level: 1st grade.
Donor: anonymous.

_____. *Rides and Slides: The Alice and Jerry Books.* Row, Peterson, 1936, 1941.
[Same as the 1936 edition, except some pictures updated in the 1941 version.]
Level: 1st grade.
Donor: anonymous.

Spelling

Aiton, G. *The Descriptive Speller for Graded and Ungraded Schools.* Boston: Ginn, 1901.
[Excellent for the one room school; a student could work independently at whatever grade level fit that child.]
Level: 3rd to 8th grades.
Donor: anonymous.

Hicks, W. *Champion Spelling Book for Public and Private Schools: Part One.* New York, Cincinnati, Chicago: American Book, 1909.
[In *Part One* and *Part Two* (below), emphasis is on drill, syllabication, and pronunciation marks. Focus on preparation for spelling contests, which were popular in that era.]
Level: 1st to 4th grades.
Donor: anonymous.

_____. *Champion Spelling Book for Public and Private Schools: Part Two.* New York, Cincinnati, Chicago: American Book, 1909.
Level: 5th to 8th grades.
Donor: anonymous.

Wohlfarth and Rogers. *New World Speller: Grades Six, Seven and Eight.* Yonkers-on-Hudson, New York: World Book, 1910.
[Study directions provided on each page to stimulate self-directed study. Drill and spelling contests emphasized.]
Level: 6th to 8th grades.
Donor: Julia Balcomb.

Index

O

Okanogan country, 1, 11, 83
Olmstead-Smith Collection, 37
Olympia, 1, 10, 14–15
Orthography, 160
Osborn family, 53

PQ

Padavich, Mary, 121
Panic of 1893, 15
Peoh Point School, 119–20
Peshastin locality, 1, 8
Peterson, Antone, 135
Peterson, Elsie, 135
Preparatory school, 20
President Black (WSNS), 21, 72
President Wilson (WSNS), 21, 71
Progressive Movement, 35
Prohibition, 18
PTA, 141
Puget Sound Power and Light, 13
Pullman, 20, 113
Quincy flats, 50

R

rattlesnakes, 44, 48, 61, 94
Reecer Creek, 147
Reed cabin, 11
Reed School, 7
Richards, Charlie, 69
Richards, Elizabeth, 67
Robber's Roost, 6
Roberts, Bynum, 93
Roberts, Mary, 91, 93
Robinson canyon, 65
Robinson, Frank and John, 127
Rolinger School, 116
Ronald, 135, 141
    schools, 135, 138, 140–41
Roslyn, 11, 15
    schools, 16
Rothrock, Cort, 54–55
Rothrock family, 52, 55
Rothrock, Frank, 42
Roza School, 90–95
Rural Training Program, 64
Rules for Teachers, 25, 171–73

S

Sabin, Mrs., 80–81
Saxby, Ethel Robinson, 127–36, 140
scarlet fever, 75
school busses/wagons, 29, 64, 107–8, 111, 119–20, 143

Schnebly Brothers, 42
Schnebly, D.D., 74
Schnebly, Elsie Hodgson, 18, 24, 28, 30, 39–57
Schnebly, Frank, 50
Schnebly, P.H., 42
Selah schools, 101
shock and awe, 34
Shoudy, John, 6, 13
Shultz, Andy, 65
Siks, Geraldine Brain, 22
silica mills, 92, 93, 94
smallpox, 75, 124
Smith, Leta May, 37, 120
smoking, 25, 77, 101
Smyser, Professor, 71, 144
Snipes, Ben, 8, 15
Snoqualmie Pass, 5, 8, 17, 18
socialists, 46–47, 51
Spanish-American War, 17
Spanish Flu, 26, 74–75, 121
spelling contests, 32, 60, 62, 73, 90
Splawn, A.J., 1, 5, 6
Splawn, Charles, 4, 5
Splawn, Viola, 4, 5
Stadtler, Stella, 21
Stampede Pass, 10–11
State of Washington Teachers' Examinations, 157–70
Stephens, William, 22, 65, 71, 127
Stepp School, 8
Sunset School, 24, 42, 52–54
Sunset Telephone and Telegraph Company, 28
Swauk locality, 7–8, 65
Sybil, Mrs., 96

T

Taneum Creek, 5
Tarpiscan, 18, 24, 43–44, 52
Tarpiscan School, 39–42, 46–48, 51
Teachers Institute, 101
Teanaway area, 134
telephones, 17, 28, 52, 55, 61
Thorp, 65
    schools, 29
Thorp, F.M., 4, 5
Thrall, 91, 95
Tonasket, 83
Town Ditch, 17
Training School, 21, 22, 59, 66
Trinidad, 53

UV

Umptaneum Falls, 69
Umptanum School, 26
University of Washington, 20, 65

The Author

Barb Owen

I grew up in Milwaukee, Wisconsin, but my imagination dwelt in the country. A summer spent on a farm at age 10, my mother's tales of my Norwegian grandfather homesteading in a sod cabin on the Dakota prairie, and reading the *Little House* books by Laura Ingalls Wilder (1867–1957) left images that have intrigued me throughout my life.

A university degree in 1953, followed by two semesters of education credits in 1961, led to a teaching certificate. From 1965 to 1970, I taught first grade at the Denmark School, six miles east of Ellensburg in rural Kittitas County. When that school closed, I taught in the town of Kittitas for many years, retiring in 1991.

Denmark was a four room school—one room for each grade, first through fourth. It was a lovely old brick building, with a gym and huge playground surrounded by farmers' fields. We held Christmas and springtime programs, and an end of school picnic, events that were entirely new experiences for a city girl like me.

In 1998, I began collecting accounts from teachers, describing their experiences in the old country schools. Now, thanks to the talented and dedicated staff at the Washington State University Press, these wonderful stories of a bygone era can be read and enjoyed by people everywhere.